Critical Acclaim for the Got, Not Got/Lost World of Football series...

Runner-up, Best Football Book, British Sports Book Awards 2012:
Got, Not Got: The A-Z of Lost Football Culture, Treasures & Pleasures.

"A veritable Dundee cake of a book."
Danny Kelly, talkSport

"Recalling a more innocent time before Sky Sports and millionaire players, *Got, Not Got* is like a long soak in a warm bath of football nostalgia: an A-Z of memorabilia, ephemera and ill-advised haircuts."
Mail on Sunday

"The real magic is the collection and display of the illustrative material of stickers, badges, programme covers, Subbuteo figures and other ephemera. It is astonishingly thorough, well-presented, inspired and indeed had me going, 'yes, got, got, not got, forgot, never seen'."
When Saturday Comes

"A cracking book which whisks you back to a different footballing era."
Brian Reade, Daily Mirror

"This memorabilia fest is a delightful reminder of what's gone from the game: 'magic sponges', Subbuteo and, er, magazines for shinpads. Such innocent times, eh?"
FourFourTwo

"The book's great fun. It's an essential if you grew up watching football in the 60s, 70s or 80s. It's a kind of football fan's catnip. Nobody can quite walk past it. They start looking at it and then realise they've got something else they should be doing 10 or 15 minutes later."
Paul Hawksbee, talkSport

"A body of work that transcends being 'just a book' by a considerable distance."
In Bed With Maradona

"There's something for every fan of every club. The authors have put so much into this book – it's a mixture of remarkable photographs, toys, stickers, club icons, and not forgetting the writing – it's beautiful!"
Andy Jacobs, talkSport

"A must-have for fans, a sought-after stocking filler."
Mirror.co.uk

"Exquisite, a celebration of football's wider culture. Regardless of whether it really was a golden age, this is a golden volume, as much a social history as a sports book. If you've not got *Got, Not Got*, you've got to get it."
Backpass

"A hugely evocative pictorial memorial to the innocence of a game before it became a business. Each page filled with the iconic paraphernalia of a homespun fandom that shaped a generation's adolescence but allowed us the space to make our own dreams."
The Morning Star

"There's a whole series of books called *Got, Not Got*: brilliant books looking back at old football memorabilia. You need them in your life. It's like finding your old football stickers."
James Brown, talkSport/Sabotage Times

"The best book about football written in the last 20 years."
Bill Borrows, Esquire

GLOVE STORY

The Number 1 book for every goalkeeper, past and present

Rob Stokes, Derek Hammond & Gary Silke

with illustrations by Doug Nash

CONKER

willow

special days for seriously ill young adults

Conker Editions Ltd
22 Cosby Road
Littlethorpe
Leicester
LE19 2HF
Email: books@conkereditions.co.uk
Website: www.conkereditions.co.uk
First published by Conker Editions Ltd 2017

A CIP catalogue record for this book is available from the British Library.
13-digit ISBN: 9781999900809
Design and typesetting by Gary Silke.
Printed in the UK by Mixam.

*"You have to be slightly mental, I think. After all, you have selected
a job which is like being a 'tail-end Charlie' in a bomber.
You're there to be shot at."*
John Osborne, West Bromwich Albion

*"People say goalkeepers are mad, but I've always thought it was the
other way round. At least the ball comes to us, whereas the outfield
players have to chase it around like idiots."*
Steve Ogrizovic, Coventry City

INTRODUCTION

I never really wanted to be a goalkeeper. I wanted to be a centre-forward, but as my elder brother had already bagged that position I was left to act as cannon fodder for his shooting practice. Our five-year age gap led to a solid grounding in the basics. If I actually managed to stop one of his shots, it saved me from having to run 50 yards to fetch the ball. Seldom did we find anywhere to play with the luxury of goal nets.

I was first selected for my school team aged nine, as a

those years of keeping my brother happy must have attributed something. Whatever reason he alighted on, whatever hidden possibilities he discerned, I must now tip my hat to Mr Ralphs, the man responsible for shaping my entire footballing life from that point on.

My first game in goal saw me wear my first ever pair of goalkeeper gloves – or, more accurately, a pair of old gardening gloves that my dad had found in the garage. To me, they weren't gloves designed for pruning roses, these were gloves in which I could emulate the keepers on *Match of the Day*. I don't have a clue how I played in that first game but I do know we won 5-1 against Fernhurst School, and that I never again played out on pitch. By process of elimination, I must have done all right – or maybe Mr Ralphs just couldn't find anyone else daft enough to go in goal

right winger, but after just one game the manager decided on a tactical switch. Thanks to my all-round sparkling ball skills and deceptive pace, he suggested I'd be better suited to a position more appropriate to my talents – in goal, out of the way.

Why he chose me as goalkeeper was beyond me. I wasn't the tallest by any means and don't remember ever showing any signs of being the next Gordon Banks, but I guess

for the rest of that term. I was a year younger than the other lads, so it wasn't just the manager I was trying to impress but also the rest of the boys who probably didn't share Mr Ralphs' mystical belief. I think I won them

8

over in the end. It must have been the gloves.

Now I was part of the Keepers' Union, watching football matches was never the same again. I wasn't interested in seeing the likes of Bobby Doyle or Billy Rafferty perform artistry on the lush green turf of Fratton Park, I was more concerned with how Peter Mellor or Alan Knight or their opposite number played – and, just as importantly,

what gloves they were wearing. My local sports shop in Drayton (the aptly named Drayton Sports, funnily enough) did stock goal-keeping gloves, but not the type the professionals wore. For a while I had to make do with green cotton gloves and the yellow-and-green table-tennis design endorsed by Peter Bonetti. They were a giant step up from the Percy Thrower gloves, granted, but they didn't even vaguely resemble the gloves I could see from the terraces, or the ones I caught tantalising glimpses of on *Match of the Day*.

Luckily for me and thousands of other junior shotstoppers, a timely advert then appeared in *Shoot!* magazine which was

9

The world's priciest keeper saves with Sukan.

destined to take goalkeeping in this country to a different level. It was the issue dated 8th December 1979. There on page 47, just beneath an article about a 'Rovers Return for Alan Warboys', was an illustration of five perfectly drawn goalkeeper gloves and one Gordon Banks jersey. I couldn't believe my eyes. These were the actual gloves being worn by Jimmy Rimmer and his fellow pro keepers – and they were available to absolutely anyone with a cheque or postal order.

The company selling the gloves was called Sukan Sports, which I assumed to be a massive, swanky sports shop in the heart of Reading. They would have rack after rack of gloves on all four walls, and a dedicated team of sales assistants who were all part-time goalkeepers. It was only many years

later, when my dad took me on a special trip to the back-streets of Caversham, that this particular illusion was shattered. My memories of that wonderful establishment are still as fresh now as they were in the 80s – but that's a story to save for later. The five gloves in the advert ranged from a choice of a Peter Bonetti or Phil Parkes pair, starting at £1.50, through to a brand called Uhlsport – the choice of professionals – which offered three different pairs in various colours and materials with a top price of £12.50.

This meant a lot of persuasion and good behaviour was going to be needed to get a pair out of my parents. The usual tactics of doing my homework, eating all my meals and doing as I was told were upped a notch, and persistent pleas that the gloves would make me a better goalkeeper were heard on a daily basis. After over a year of relentless pressure, convincing my folks that my life was to be spent firmly between the sticks, they finally gave in.

On my eleventh birthday a pair of Uhlsport 023 gloves in size 7 were firmly planted on my tiny size 5 hands. I didn't care if they were too big, I was now a professional keeper. The best in my road. What struck me at the time was the distinct smell coming off gloves' PU velvet. It's hard to describe or to explain, but anyone who has ever owned a pair will know what I mean.

Back then, the gloves had to last from my birthday in July through to Christmas, then from Christmas to my next birthday. Sometimes, if I was lucky, I might get a pair in between. Without fail, a new pair of gloves was always top of any hopeful wants list, along with a *Roy of the Rovers* annual from one of my aunts or uncles.

One Christmas, I craftily opened up a present a few days early without my parents' knowledge, knowing a pair of gloves was going to be inside. Egged on by my brother, we took them up the park for a kickabout. Not thinking too carefully about the state of the pitches, which weren't exactly Wembley on a May afternoon, we got a little too involved in our private big match. Getting the mud off the gloves and trying to restore them to their virginal state was a tricky task. However, we managed to get them back in the box and pulled off an Oscar-worthy impression of great surprise when they were unwrapped, for a second time, a few days later.

While Sukan Sports went on to become such an important part of the goalkeeping world, adding ever more gloves and styles to their ads in *Shoot!* and *Match*, I was now on the slippery slope of a lifetime obsession. I never went on to perform in the professional game but was lucky enough to play for Waterlooville in the Southern League for eight seasons, racking up endless enjoyment and memories – and, of course, going through a huge number of different gloves along the way.

It's all a long time ago now... but once a keeper, always a keeper. In the intervening

years my collection of gloves, books, cuttings, photographs and equally enthusiastic goalkeeping contacts has grown almost out of control – with everything and everyone taking me right back to that happy place between the sticks.

Here's hoping you enjoy this celebration of goalkeeping – the stories, the legends, the treasures and pleasures – and everything it means to pull on a large pair of luminous latex gloves.

11

CLUTCHING THE BALL

When you've given up an hour and a half of your own time and selflessly devoted it to preventing a ball flying into a net, a strange feeling can come over you when you actually get the ball in your hands. It's a profound feeling. A primordial urge that dates back to when Stonehenge was used as goalposts.

EVERTON

GORDON WEST
GOAL KEEPER

Your team-mates are yelling at you to throw the ball to them, but you pretend you haven't heard. Part of you is tempted to boot it as far as possible down the other end of the pitch, away from danger. But, just for a moment or two, it's a wonderful feeling to just clutch the ball to your chest, safely out of harm's way.

"Goalie's ball!" you bellowed optimistically as the cross flew from

Go West: where the skies are blue.

the wing into your area. And now it really is yours, you're going to cling on to it for as long as humanly

gordon marshall

Goalkeeper   HEARTS

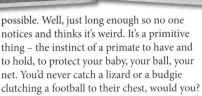

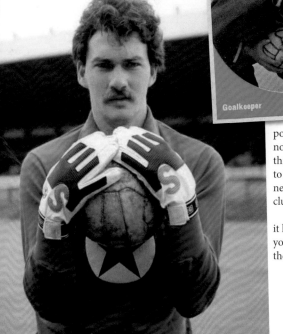

possible. Well, just long enough so no one notices and thinks it's weird. It's a primitive thing – the instinct of a primate to have and to hold, to protect your baby, your ball, your net. You'd never catch a lizard or a budgie clutching a football to their chest, would you?

So clasp the ball to your chest and cuddle it hard. Watch the oppo try and score while you've got your whole body wrapped around the ball. No one will ever get it off you. Ha!

Big Nev oversees Little Paul Owens' clutching practise.

GOALIE SHIRT EVOLUTION

While the goalkeeper always had handling privileges, initially anywhere on the pitch, it wasn't until 1909 that the authorities thought to mark him out by way of a different jersey colour. At the Football League's AGM in June of that year, it was decided that the keeper should wear either scarlet, blue or white,

but these three colours were the most common team colours and so in 1912 green was added as an option, quickly coming to prominence given the lack of need for an alternative.

In 1921, the International Football Association sought to set aside a colour for countries' goalkeeper shirts – the FA proposed red but their FAW counterparts unsurprisingly took issue with this and so yellow was settled upon. Yellow would also become common in Scotland, given that green featured more north of the border.

From there, for so long, it was so simple in English football – the two goalkeepers wore plain green jerseys and the same shorts and socks as their team-mates, a law which would later put an end to Peter Bonetti's experiment with all-green kit.

The early 20th century had seen goalkeepers wear heavy woollen roll-neck shirts, and it has gone down in folklore that Arsenal goalkeeper Dan Lewis blamed the shininess of his new top for the goal which saw Cardiff City win the 1927 FA Cup final. Thereafter, Arsenal would always wash the new shirt before a Cup final, until Bob Wilson was allowed to wear one fresh from its packaging in 1971.

The Football League rules stated that the GK shirts had to be 'self-coloured', ie lacking in any extra detailing or colours, though Peter Shilton still

managed to get his signature shirts banned on the strength of their 'dangerous' zip. Meanwhile, Peter Bonetti's green tops with

Reusch Polyester jersey, with padded elbows and No.1 on both front and back.

available in numerous colours such as yellow, blue, red, green and orange, a black upper panel and sleeves were common to all. Conservatism among the English authorities was still evident in that, while this Adidas design was worn by Ipswich goalkeeper Paul Cooper in the 1981 UEFA Cup final, he was still restricted to solid-colour offerings domestically.

Sondico **Ray Clemence** polyester jersey, with padded elbow and No.1 on the back.

black trim were used for a couple of years before they were banned by the Football League. Shilton, spotting another marketing opportunity, then opted to turn out in all white – permitted, but worn by few others.

By then, there had been an unresisted move by some clubs to the same stripy crew necks which featured on outfield shirts, and flappy collars began to become popular in the 70s, also the decade in which branding began to creep in.

Admiral's big marketing push in the UK saw bespoke designs come in on outfield shirts and when they secured the England team contract the big change for the goalkeeper's outfit was that it became a distinct kit – black shorts and socks now complementing the yellow shirt, with contrast stripes down the sleeves.

Keen to keep pace with Admiral, Adidas added their own markings to kits too and in the late 70s they made what was, at the time, the most radical move in goalkeeper designs with the launch of a 'dip-dye' style shirt -

A sub-genre was that many goalkeepers preferred to wear shirts produced by the glove companies, such as Uhlsport, Reusch and Sondico, as they offered superior padding and protection. As kit contracts began to become bigger business, this practice disappeared.

Design elements began to creep in during the 1980s as manufacturers added subtle shadow stripes and discreet trim. All previous restrictions on colours and styles were withdrawn during the summer of 1985, so for the 1985-86 season and onwards anything went, providing the referee was happy that there was no colour clash with outfield players.

In retrospect, the 1990 World Cup was perhaps the hinge point between the old and new goalkeeping kit worlds. While many netminders had classic looks, others had outfits which, shall we say, tested artistic sensibilities. And that was only the start of it...

Umbro Internationale shiny polyester jersey with pin stripe front panel, padded elbows and No.1 on the back.

Adidas Two Tone shiny polyester/cotton jersey, with padded elbows and No.1 on the back.

15

PREHISTORY

It's all aboard the Glove Story rollercoaster for a lightning-fast timeline tour through the history of football from the unique perspective of the goal-line.

You'll notice we didn't say 'from the goal area' there, or even 'from the goal', because such developments, at least as we know them, came long after football came kicking and screaming into the world. In the mid 19th century, the trendy new game was a hybrid of the anarchic mass 'folk football' matches played across hilltops and through town centres up and down England, together with the distinctly militaristic kick-and-charge ball

Goalkeepers' Gloves

No. 61 **Yellow Chamois,** buttoned and ventilated.
No. 62 **Ditto,** rubber palms.
No. 63 **Ditto,** rubber palms and backs.
No. 64 **Gold Cape,** buttoned and ventilated, very strong.
No. 65 **Ditto,** rubbered palms.
No. 66 **Ditto,** rubbered palms and backs.
No. 67 **Best Gold Cape,** rubbered palms and backs, a splendid wearing glove.

Gallaher's Cigarettes.

game played at public schools and universities.

1863 In the year the Football Association was formed, team tactics were relatively easy to plan as every team was made up of nine forwards and two behinds. No goalkeeper. Which was probably just as well, because the goal itself was barely recognisable as such.

1867 The laws of the game stated: "A goal shall be won when the ball passes between the goalposts under the tape, not being thrown, knocked on, or carried."

1871 Goalkeepers now officially appeared in the laws of the game, empowered to handle the ball anywhere inside their own half. In the previous eight years the Fair Catch rule had allowed any player to catch the ball and, provided they made a mark in the pitch with their boot, win a free kick. They still get up to these prehistoric tricks in rugby. But football

Gallaher's Cigarettes.

What It Feels Like—Keeping Goal for the First Time

never permitted players to run with the ball in their hands, nor score from a throw.

1875 Goalposts topped with tape were replaced with a crossbar – a law made compulsory in **1882**. It's strangely gratifying to discover that goalkeepers made their mark so quickly, causing a major change in the playing area's key equipment. Crossbars were introduced because of the cunning goalie's knack of tugging down on the old tape, and casually watching shots go sailing over.

1891 Goal nets were finally introduced, supplied by the manufacturers Brodie of Liverpool, thus ending all possible goal disputes. Or so they thought...

1894 Up until this point, goalies were fair game for charging, pushing and shoving at any point in the game; but now they could only be bashed about or knocked senseless when an outfield player was playing the ball or obstructing an opponent.

1895 Having alighted on the masterstroke of a goal frame with a crossbar, the FA at last decided to standardise their width – not more than five inches. The mind boggles at the previous possibilities.

1909 Up until now, goalkeepers had worn exactly the same kit as their team-mates. The introduction of special keepers' uniforms came with an optional flat cap chucked in for free.

1912 The goalkeeper's use of his hands was now restricted to the penalty area, reining in his special powers previously enjoyed all the way up to the half-way line. The following year saw the introduction of the 10-yard limit for players to retreat at a free-kick: drat, it must have been easy lining up your wall when it was only four inches from the ball.

1929 In the same way, the penalty-kick must have posed a very different threat before the law was introduced compelling a goalie to stay on his line.

1931 In their wisdom the Powers that Be now generously decided to let a goalkeeper take four steps in possession of the ball, double the previous rather skinny allowance of two.

1936 Up until just before WWII, a defender was allowed to take a goal-kick and simply tap it into the goalie's hands. This may not seem such a big deal in an era when a goalkeeper can kick a dead ball the length of the field; but back in the days of heavy leather balls and boots it took a drop-kick from the hands on the edge of the penalty box to get the ball into the oppo's half.

And so ended the prehistoric era of goalkeeping. After the war, keepers started to indulge for the first time in all sorts of thoroughly modern pastimes – training, wearing caps instead of flat caps, getting multi-hundred guinea endorsements for moustache oil – that soon saw the excesses of the modern era upon us.

Bring back the cross-tape!

OGDEN'S CIGARETTES.

W. FOULKE.

OGDEN'S CIGARETTES

H. HIBBS (BIRMINGHAM)

17

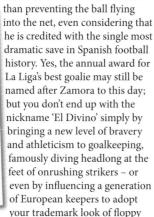

ZAMORA

Recognised as one of the all-time greats, Spanish shot-stopping superstar Ricardo Zamora extended the influence and enhanced the glamour of the goalie's role during his long inter-war career playing for Espanyol, Barcelona and Real Madrid. And we'd like to talk about his toy puppet.

There was much, much more to Zamora than preventing the ball flying into the net, even considering that he is credited with the single most dramatic save in Spanish football history. Yes, the annual award for La Liga's best goalie may still be named after Zamora to this day; but you don't end up with the nickname 'El Divino' simply by bringing a new level of bravery and athleticism to goalkeeping, famously diving headlong at the feet of onrushing strikers – or even by influencing a generation of European keepers to adopt your trademark look of floppy cloth cap and white polo-neck jumper.

If you throw into the mix the fact that Zamora was also an enigmatic political figure, a heavy drinker and smoker, a sex symbol 'more famous than Garbo and better looking', and the first and most controversial big-money signing ever made by Real Madrid, you start to draw closer to the basis of his charismatic cult.

Born in Catalonia to Spanish parents, Zamora was neck deep in the nationalist controversies which led up to the Spanish Civil War. When the one-time Barcelona star was signed by the rising power of Real Madrid in 1930, it caused even greater ructions than it would today. On the eve of war, in 1936, the two deadly rivals faced each other in the Spanish Cup final, in what must have been the most tense *clásico* of all. With the score

at 2-1 with three minutes to go, Barcelona striker Josep Escolà collected a ball from the right and hit a shot hard and low, apparently beyond Zamora's reach. All the crowd saw was a great cloud of dust as Zamora took off in the bare goalmouth, as the goal celebrations began. Only when the dust settled did they see, not the ball in the back of the net, but Zamora standing coolly with the ball cradled in his arms.

It may come as little surprise to hear that, just months later, Spanish newspapers reported Zamora had been found shot dead in a Madrid gutter, his body peppered with bullets. Yet such was Zamora's mystique, no one knew whether to blame the fascists or the leftists. As it turned out, the report was false. Zamora was instead arrested by militiamen and could have faced execution, but he charmed them by playing penalties and eventually escaped.

The Zamora story isn't a page, it's a movie. And we can't wait for it to be made, if only to find out more about that mysterious puppet!

The great Zamora manfully ignores his naughty puppet.

18

BOG ROLL & OTHER MISSILES

Back in the good old days, a visiting goalkeeper was always guaranteed a polite, if not actually rousing, round of applause from home fans when he trotted into his goalmouth at the beginning of the halves. As if to balance this wilful nugget of selective rose-tinted memory, applause wasn't the only thing that fans on the terraces had in store for the keeper.

Goodness knows what a Premier League Health & Safety Officer would make of the age-old tradition of showering the goal, the goalkeeper and any other inviting target with toilet paper rolls when a goal went in. It was a curious spectacle with a potential for a graceful, quite beautiful arc if a loo roll were thrown with the requisite backspin from the back of the Kop or, better still, from the Double Decker. Though it wasn't quite so welcome from a goalie's perspective, signalling failure and humiliation.

It could have been worse, and indeed often was. The unique vulnerability of the goalkeeper – forced to stand just a few yards in front of a baying heap of 10,000 partisan fans – was underlined in wintertime, especially when games went ahead with snow on the pitch and the terraces. Perhaps the most infamous example of a goalie being used for target practice occurred in January 1979, on the occasion of a third-round FA Cup tie between Sheffield Wednesday and Arsenal. No one present remembers the game or the score, but rest assured Pat Jennings still recalls with crystal clarity the continual barrage of snowballs aimed at his back.

Mercifully, there were very few incidents where weapons more offensive than snow were thrown at keepers, but Big Pat and Phil Parkes were just two victims of darts during the darkest days of holiganism.

If you think things couldn't possibly have descended further, you've failed to factor in two elements: 1) a small group of Millwall fans back in the 1960s, and b) their obsessive, excessive antagonism towards any goalie deemed a 'Flash 'Arry' – aka a keeper would

delight in winding up the oppo fans.

There was no cooler, cockier Flash 'Arry than Brentford's Chic Brodie – and so a plot was hatched to put the wind up the Bees' goalie with the aid of a prop discovered in an Isle of Dogs garden toolshed. That Saturday afternoon, amid the usual hail of coins and bog roll, an unexpected foreign object rolled out into the Brentford penalty-box. 'HAND GRENADE SHOCKS SOCCER', screamed the *Daily Sketch* the next day.

Ah yes, the good old days.

Soft, strong and very long: Spurs' Ian Walker.

FIRST GLOVE

Jordan Pickford

"I was six years old at the time and my father bought me a cheap pair of Reusch gloves, because I wanted to be just like my hero Peter Schmeichel.**"**

19

The Greatest SAVES **No 1**

GORDON BANKS
ENGLAND 0-1 BRAZIL
Date: 7 June 1970
Venue: Estadio Jalisco, Mexico

It was still 0-0 after 18 minutes in the Clash of the Titans group match at Mexico 70. Jairzinho broke free down the right, powered past Terry Cooper to the by-line and looped over a cross to the back post, completely cutting out Moore, Labone and Mullery. Pele was lurking, springing high above right-back Tommy Wright to head the ball powerfully down toward the bottom left-hand corner of the net. Banks threw himself instinctively sideways and backwards into the corner, but in that fraction of a second it was all too clear he didn't have a cat in hell's chance. One-nil to the samba stars against the reigning world champions. Pele reeled away in celebration.

"I heard Pele shout 'goal' as he headed it," Banks later recalled, "which was followed by a massive, almost deafening roar. Even though I'd got a hand to it, I thought he must have scored."

But of course Banks had not only reached the ball off the goal-line but somehow clawed it directly up and over the crossbar by no more than four or five inches...

"Then I realised. The crowd were cheering for me."

What a save... GORDON BANKS

BOOTS FOR GOALIES

It's a vexed subject, specialist boots for goalkeepers. They're either a pointless gimmick or an attractive extra option, dependent on your point of view. In this respect, they're very much akin to the controversial coloured football boots, topic of which are now pretty much the norm in the pro game – much to the chagrin of the football traditionalists. So let's grasp the bull by the horns and introduce what was perhaps the ultimate wind-up in football footwear: an historic pair of coloured boots for goalies.

It was Alan Ball who started off the trend for flashy white boots, marketed by Hummel along with the red pair occasionally sported by Charlie George. And here's proof that Banks of England was also at the cutting edge of footballing fashion in 1972. As the advert from *Goal* magazine states, they're Top Quality

Gordon Banks on Kingswell

Kingswell Soccer Boots are now exclusively worn and recommended by Gordon Banks, the world's leading goalkeeper and footballer of the year, Peter Lorimer, the Leeds striker, reputed to have the hardest shot in soccer, and other leading professionals. See the Kingswell range at your local sports retailers. Illustrated: 650 Avenger. The latest styling with distinctive stripes. Real hide uppers with multi-studded moulded soles. Recommended retail £3·99. 675/1 Mexico. Top quality black calf uppers, thickly padded, with distinctive red & white stripes. Polyurethane soles with screw-in nylon studs. Recommended retail £6·50. GB1 Gordon Banks. A new colourful boot with soft red hide uppers and white moulded rubber soles. Recommended retail from £2·88 to £3·75

Kingswell Shoe Co., Cliftonville Road, Northampton NN1 5EG
Tel 21744/5/6 (3 lines) 24 hour answering service on 21744 **Kingswell**

Leather, recommended and autographed by Gordon himself. The real problem with these Kingswell Bobby Dazzlers is that there are no features or benefits aimed specifically at goalies. That's why Banks never wore the boots himself!

It wasn't until 1998 that Uhlsport launched the goalie-friendly Temac No.1 boot, with a raised heel and small studs on the edge of the sole to assist with lateral movement, exclusively endorsed by Tim Flowers.

I even bought a pair of these when they came out, but the tiny design changes made very little difference in reality. The steady flow of goals conceded remained alarmingly consistent. I might have been better off wearing them on my hands.

In the red: Banks of England.

21

GLOVEBAGS

Once upon a time the glovebag was every keeper's favourite comfort blanket, though these handy, lucky, deeply personal objects of obsession disappeared from the back of the nation's goalnets around the late 90s. So much for the must-have fashion accessory that saw goalies cross the white line with countless pairs of gloves overflowing from their accessory bag along with lucky charms and personal mementoes.

On occasion, Jimmy Rimmer could even be seen with two glovebags due to the vast amount of gloves he liked to have with him. Now that's what we call one-upmanship. The question why they died out is a tricky one to answer. For starters, pitches became much more reliable so there wasn't the need to carry so many different pairs because of the clinging mud that forced a fresh pair to be plucked out.

In his goalkeeping guide *In Search of Perfection*, Neville Southall tellingly stated: "I don't take a glovebag out with me that often now – it gives the opposition something to aim at." Phil Parkes (of QPR and West Ham) was of the same view, but then he had previously chosen to stash his glovebag just behind the goal line right in the centre of the goal – perhaps without realising he was literally throwing down the gauntlet!

With the introduction of ever more substitutes, coaching and medical staff on the bench, spare gloves now often tend to be left in the care of one of the retinue – the kitman, most obviously – rather than be taken on to the pitch. And then there's the age-old problem of the bag getting swiped, which didn't only apply to parks goalies. Alan Knight of Portsmouth lost one to a light-fingered fan who hurdled the hoardings at Huddersfield,

SUKAN PVC GLOVE BAG
£1.50

REUSCH PVC GLOVE BAG
£3.30

SONDICO RED PVC GLOVE BAG
£3.40

SONDICO BLUE PVC GLOVE BAG
£3.40

UHL NYLON GLOVE BAG
£3.75

MITRE NYLON GLOVE BAG
£3.99

DATE

TECHNICAL DATA

back in October 1982. If the culprit is reading this, he says he'd like it back!

The earliest production glovebag was first used by the inseparable Peter Shilton and Ray Clemence, a black-and-white number manufactured by Sondico Sports. This was originally the same style of bag that the company used for table tennis bats. Mr Sondhi was ever alert to an opportunity to advertise his products, adding branding to the

Gunn revealed that together with the bare essentials of spare gloves and a cap, he kept a locket with a picture of his daughter Francesca and a strand of her hair; also a pair of pink Uhlsport gloves that were specially made for her. John Burridge told us that he used to carry with him seven or eight different styles of gloves, so that he was ready with a pair to suit any conditions. Having taken the question to Twitter, Stuart Page passed on a top tip: in the winter months, he carried surgical gloves to wear underneath his regular pair and keep his hands dry and warm. "A Panini sticker of Ray Clemence," Carl Alexander answered, "as he wore the same gloves I was wearing, and I thought it might bring some good luck."

front and back.

Before this development, keepers would carry a spare pair of gloves inside their cap or, if you were Pat Jennings, a suitable silver polythene carrier bag would work just fine. It's unclear whether a deal with Tesco was ever considered, but he would certainly have guaranteed them some great exposure during the 82 and 86 World Cup Finals. Interestingly, Jennings used to keep in his bag the prayer of St Jude. The patron saint of lost causes.

We asked lots of other keepers about the secret contents of their glovebags. Bryan

Finally, we asked Barrie Tomlinson, legendary editor of *Roy of the Rovers*, about the little skeleton called Fred that Gordon 'The Safest Hands in Soccer' Stewart kept in his glovebag. "It used to bring him luck," Barrie replied. "Make no bones about it!"

GOALIES WITHOUT GLOVES

In the days before modern goalkeeping gloves, keepers relied on their bare hands along with just a bit of spittle. Cotton gloves were an option in wet weather but, when it was dry, there was an extra ingredient that gave your spit a magical property.

"I can recall playing with bare hands," Dave Beasant told us, "and chewing gum – so when you spat on your hands in dry weather, it would give a tacky feel!"

As a gloveless goalie, David Icke had an alternative to Beech Nut chewy – a quick scrub of lemon juice. You might think it sounds a suitably barking idea, until you realise it was a tip passed on by the great Wolves and England goalie, Bert Williams. The goalie-*cum*-newsreader turned global conspiracy theorist let it slip when hosting *Saturday Superstore* in 1982, while he was talking gloves with Ray

Clemence of Tottenham and England.

Judging by the state of ex-Burnley and Fulham keeper Peter Mellor's fingers, which suffered in the gloveless age, it's definitely worth grabbing all the protection that gloves offer. But try telling that to Simon Farnworth (of Bolton, Bury, Preston and Wigan fame) who goes down as the very last of the gloveless wonders.

"Right up until I finished playing in 1996 I

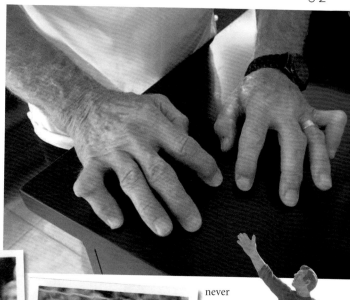

Going gloveless: Peter Mellor paid the price.

never wore any gloves in dry weather," Simon confirmed when we spoke to him. "Unless it was on the plastic pitch of Preston." Ironically, Simon then became a physio, and Football League rules demanded he wore surgical gloves when treating players on the pitch!

25

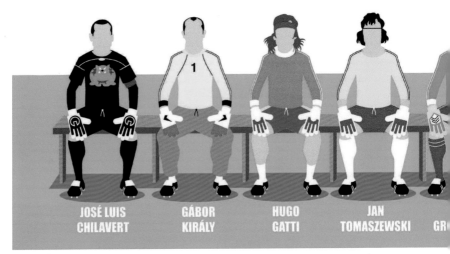

JOSÉ LUIS CHILAVERT GÁBOR KIRÁLY HUGO GATTI JAN TOMASZEWSKI GR

GOALKEEPERS ARE CRAZY

"I have always held it to be axiomatic that goalkeepers have a slate loose," pronounced *The Times*' football writer, Geoffrey Green. But is it objectively true that goalkeepers are crazy? There's certainly hard evidence to suggest that at least nine were a couple of sandwiches short of a picnic...

José Luis Chilavert

Spot the inspirational giant with the cartoon bulldog emblazoned on his jersey – brawling, racing out of goal with the ball at his feet, howling like a wolf and clapping furiously after every successful save, sliding on his chest in celebration of every goal. And, yes, there were plenty of goals from Chilavert – a staggering 54 in total – mostly free-kicks drilled with sublime accuracy and power from literally anywhere on the pitch. Such lavish outfield skills, showboating and brazen eccentricity are almost enough to make you forget the Paraguayan claimed the title of World's Best Goalkeeper of the Year three times.

Gábor Király

"How could he not be a cult hero, this Bon Jovi-loving, Mini-driving, roly-poly performing, muddy-kneed goalkeeper with the hint of a belly, whose career stretches all the way back to the last century and takes in Haladas and Hertha Berlin, Crystal Palace and Aston Villa, Burnley and Bayer Leverkusen? The man who had Fulham fans turning up to games in his tracksuit bottoms and 1860 Munich's club shop selling them?"
– Sid Lowe, *The Guardian*, 2016

Hugo Gatti

"Boca Juniors and Argentina goalkeeper Hugo Gatti is probably right when he claims he was victimised by the Argentinian authorities. Colourful character Gatti keeps his long hair out of his eyes by wearing a headband, so the FA took it into their heads to ban him for wearing 'a dangerous garment not specified in the regulations.'" – *Shoot!*, 1977. Another brave but ultimately failed attempt by the AFA to rid themselves of their recurrent problem. A goalie who would impulsively dribble out of defence, take on opposition players and continue right on into the attack. Wearing a trademark headband, of course. And an 'L' for 'El Loco' on his jersey.

Jan Tomaszewski

"A circus clown in gloves." – Brian Clough. "He hurled himself arms, knees and bumps-a-daisy all over his penalty area like a slackly strung marionette – and all with a half-taunting, half-surprised smile which made one think this might be his first-ever game." – Frank Keating, *The Guardian*. And the final score?

Bruce Grobbelaar

"Trained to kill, Grobbelaar can't wait to be in the firing line. He wants to represent Zimbabwe in the World Cup finals and his other ambition is even more unlikely. He hopes to take up professional baseball when his soccer

PETAR
BOROTA

JORGE
CAMPOS

JOHN
BURRIDGE

RAMÓN
QUIROGA

career is completed! The Liverpool bachelor has certainly come a long way since dodging the bullets in the khaki battledress of the Rhodesian Army." – *Shoot!*, 1981

Was the infamous 'spaghetti-legs' trick one of several too many low points in the career of a chancer, a miscast dreamer? Are distraction techniques ever warranted weapons in the keeper's armoury? Did Liverpool beat Roma to become European champions in 1984?

Petar Borota

"Certainly Borota was unorthodox. The swashbuckler from Belgrade was ready to indulge in a whole range of extravagant manoeuvres. Often he would dash from his box to make a clearance or attempt to dribble past an opponent, not always with marked success; he was known to head crosses clear instead of catching or punching them; he would swing on his crossbar; and one particularly provocative party-piece was deliberately bouncing the ball off his own bar when he judged the proceedings to be a trifle dull." – Obituaries, *The Independent*, 2010

Jorge Campos

The Mexican keeper lit up the 1994 and 1998 World Cups like a psychedelic banana, having started out playing up front for Pumas UNAM (scoring 31 goals in his initial seven-year as a striker), and never quite managed to remember that he was supposed to have switched positions to become a full-time goalie. The world has seen many acrobatic, flamboyant and insanely attack-minded

keepers; but only one who was self-conscious about standing 5'8" as a goalie – and so used to stand on a ball in team groups.

John Burridge

Workington, Blackpool, Aston Villa, Southend United (loan), Crystal Palace, QPR, Wolves, Derby County (loan), Sheffield United, Southampton, Newcastle United, Hibernian, Newcastle United, Scarborough, Lincoln City, Enfield, Aberdeen, Newcastle United, Dunfermline Athletic, Dumbarton, Falkirk, Manchester City, Notts County, Witton Albion, Darlington, Grimsby Town, Gateshead, Northampton Town, Queen of the South, Purfleet, Blyth Spartans, Scarborough, Blyth Spartans.

1969-97, 768 League appearances.

Ramón Quiroga

Shared the nickname 'El Loco' with Hugo Gatti at the 1978 World Cup, where the pair set the benchmark for the specialist South American position of eccentric, wandering stopper. In order to sample some prime-time Quiroga, just Google 'Mad Peru goalkeeper'. Inside a mere 28 seconds, it's possible to feel a certain sympathy for the Polish forward who runs on to a through-ball 40 yards from goal, only to be surprised by a waist-high tackle from the meandering keeper. The sentiment kicks in even more strongly when Grzegorz Lato picks up the ball on the break, 10 yards inside his own half – only to find his progress hampered by the lurking Peruvian keeper, who drags him bodily to the ground.

LOOKING AFTER NUMBER 1

Goalie Endorsements

No 1 - Pat **Jennings**

Of all the strange and wonderful products that goalies have lent their names to over the years, Pat Jennings holds a special place in our affections for the eccentric singularity of his choices.

Imagine the scene, when a representative from the car industry turned up at Spurs' Cheshunt training ground and asked for a quiet word with the big man. What dreams of glamour and riches must have rushed through his mind as he put down the two balls he was holding effortlessly in his hands and walked in his muddy tracky bottoms to the well-appointed tea hut.

Pat would have eyed up the man from the motor trade, hopeful of spotting a Lamborghini badge on his briefcase, or perhaps

Oil be back: Big Pat rocks the oil filter look.

a Bentley key ring tossed nonchalantly by his cuppa.

"So..." Pat would doubtless have looked on the bright side once the proposition

had been outlined by the man from Unipart. "You'd like me to dress up as an oil filter? And stop a few shots? But it won't be a ball I'm saving, just big clods of muck, like?"

"An oil filter is like a goalkeeper. The more it saves, the better it is."

"And there'll be a fake crowd on the terrace behind, singing 'Unipart, cha-cha-cha'? And I won't really look much like an oil filter, more like a big reel of cotton?"

"That is correct."

"Ah, good stuff. Where do I sign?"

And that's when the marketing man casually mentioned the possibility of Pat also getting to star on a pencil sharpener in a school stationery set by Helix. Not just any pencil sharpener, mind, but one with a ball-bearing game in the top.

HANDBALL MARADONA!

Produced in 1986 by Argus Press Software, Handball Maradona enabled Commodore 64 aficionados to take complete control of legendary keeper Peter Shilton. Well, a tiny 10-pixel version of him, at any rate. For just £6.99, you had the chance to squeeze into

little Peter's microscopic gloves and attempt to save a barrage of shots from a whole team of ominously squat strikers.

Rather than aiming to simulate a whole match, the game concentrated strictly on your ability to stop shots from the edge of the box.

You first selected your teams from a rather lightweight list (which nevertheless ran to Oxford United, Oldham Athletic and Crewe Alexandra). Then, with the assistance of a couple of defenders, you faced a succession of efforts from various distances and angles.

Toggling left and right had never before seemed so much fun. The levels of sheer joy attained on Handball Maradona ruined mere real-life goalkeeping for many kids. It may have been basic, but at the time it was just as addictive as Fifa 19.

Only in retrospect does it seem a shame there's no chance to redeem England's pride; to come out and claim that miscued clearance by Steve Hodge whilst putting little Diego into Row Z.

Developed 30 years later, Handball Maradona may well have featured a custom 3D glove selection from Peter's glovebag, but they'd never have improved on that vintage

synthesizer one-finger theme tune. Check it out on YouTube – and eat your hearts out, Depeche Mode.

FIRST GLOVE

Jack Butland

"I was an outfield player till 2005, and then ended up in goal. My dad took me along to my local sports shop and he got me a cheap pair of Sondico gloves."

KARTOON KEEPERS

Every goalie of a certain age recalls the heroic graphics and the ramped-up drama centred around comic-book goalkeepers such as Peter 'The Cat' Swain, Melchester Rovers' 'Tubby' Morton or Charlie Carter, 'The Boy in the Velvet Mask', Billy 'The Fish' Thompson...

Action and melodrama were all-important, not cutting-edge realism. So who would have thought that Gordon Stewart, Tynefield City's reliable Scottish stalwart from *Roy of the Rovers*' 'The Safest Hands in Soccer', would be one of the early pioneers in bringing out his own range of gloves?

Gordon was first tempted by the promise of endorsement riches by unscrupulous agent Danny Smart back in 1979. Sadly, in a tense plot twist, the 'Gordon Stewart Specials' proved to be rubbish. However, when Gordon's son, Rick, came through the youth ranks, real-life glove baron Dave Holmes

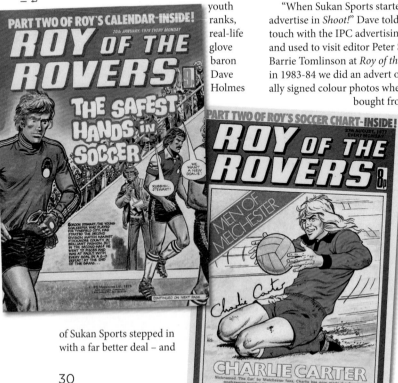

In safe hands: Gordon takes the Smart money.

a handy bit of product placement for his wares.

"When Sukan Sports started, we used to advertise in *Shoot!*" Dave told us. "I kept in touch with the IPC advertising department, and used to visit editor Peter Stewart, plus Barrie Tomlinson at *Roy of the Rovers*. And in 1983-84 we did an advert offering personally signed colour photos when a jersey was bought from us."

With Gordon Stewart's death in a Brazilian plane crash, it was time for Rick to step up. "But his gloves were drawn in a general, unbranded style," Dave recalls. "And over a period of time I thought that it

of Sukan Sports stepped in with a far better deal – and

would be good publicity if he wore Sukan/Reusch 124 'S' gloves – 'S' for Stewart, of course! The next time I saw Barrie Tomlinson I suggested this to him, and thankfully he liked the idea. I never knew who the artist was, but he certainly made a good job of showing the gloves in the storyline."

"We dropped the Sukan/Reusch gloves at the end of the 1984-85 season, and then I suggested that the gloves be changed to an Uhlsport model. Again this was agreed to with Barrie, and the first issue I have with Rick Stewart wearing Uhlsport is 23rd August 1986. *Roy of the Rovers* gave the gloves some great coverage!"

Again, it was a case of art imitating life, the gloves adding heightened realism to the comic-book storylines – one of sport's first virtual sponsorship deals in the pre-internet age.

The Bert Trautmann story is one of the most touching and dramatic chapters in the annals of postwar football history. Back in the 40s and early 50s, a war-ravaged, miserably rationed Britain still living among bomb craters just wasn't ready for a German sporting hero. It's heartwarming how Trautmann was able to soar above the demonisation and earn a place in fans' hearts – and telling how his courageous style influenced later keepers.

Even so, it wasn't the most promising start for a putative British football star, joining the Hitler Youth aged 10 – it was all "sport, sport, sport," he said – and then the Luftwaffe at 17, ending up as a paratrooper fighting in Russia.

A great practitioner of catching, Bert was also pretty good at getting caught. In the spring of 1945 he was captured by the Americans, escaped, was caught again by the British and made a Prisoner of War – a designation he

B. TRAUTMAN

retained for his first four years of his professional life.

As the star of local St Helens Town, where attendances soared during his stay, Trautmann was scouted and signed for Manchester City in October 1949. Letters of complaint flooded into local papers and thousands protested, but the players welcomed him warmly.

Before long, every kid in Manchester wanted to be like Bert. Further afield, a young Bob Wilson found himself a new hero and modelled his style on the German's. Interestingly, Bert had learned to dive as a paratrooper and had no fear of diving at opponents' feet head first, a style which Wilson carried into his own game.

In a 17-year career at City, Bert played over 500 games. He was the first goalkeeper to receive the Footballer of the Year award, in 1956, and now we can look forward to a film based on his story.

All international XI versus a combined Manchester City and Manchester United XI

Wednesday April 15th 1964
at Maine Road Manchester
kick off 7-30 p.m.

BERT TRAUTMANN

testimonial match

Official programme
one shilling

bert trautmann

Goalkeeper MANCHESTER CITY

FULLY FOCUSED

Back in the 70s, one of the chief glories of *Shoot!* magazine's 'Focus On...' pages was their heartwarming predictability. If you wanted to grow up to be a professional footballer, this solid starter course seemed to suggest that you'd first better start eating steak and chips, watching Morecambe & Wise, listening to Barry White and letting your youth-team coach influence your career.

Perhaps unsurprisingly, some of the goalies featured veered some way off the beaten track of stock responses. Did Jim Blyth really not know the correct answer ("Muhammad Ali") when he said he'd most like to meet "Jillian Duxbury of *Sun* Page Three fame"? Throw in a deep dislike of shopping with his missus, and the Cov keeper was clearly at risk of incurring his Biggest Drag in Soccer: injuries!

Likewise, Alan Rough may have fallen foul of to-day's PC police, ironically by namechecking his best mate, 'Piggy' Whittaker. However, Alan claws back some good-will with the sheer down-to-earth honesty of his alternative career. No, not a PT instructor. If he weren't the Scotland keeper, he'd probably be a pallet maker.

There were no such limitations on Gary Bailey's alternative CV. He spent his day off studying hard at university, dreaming of one day leaving behind the noise and adulation of Old Trafford to enjoy the glamorous life of a civil engineer. In true student style, Gary's taste in music ran to "Rock groups such as Jethro Tull."

It was up to the other lads to show Gary what he was missing out on: Kiki Dee and John Denver. Stevie Wonder. Barry White.

Disappointments, drags and dislikes loomed large in the lives of these 70s stars – travelling to away games, bad refs, but there were few in the whole series to compare with the heartbreak of Jim Cruickshank.

Was it really possible that Heart of

Midlothian missed out on the Scottish League championship in 1965 by five one-hundredths of a goal?

And, yes, his team-mates all secretly blamed Jim for failing to grow his fingernails a quarter of an inch longer.

Dino Zoff's best friend? "The manager of our team, Mr Bancario."

PREMIER LEAGUE INVASION

Football journalist and goalkeeping coach David Preece was in Sunderland's Youth team at the dawn of the Premier League era, already a fan of exotic foreign goalkeepers, their new styles and ways of thinking.

For David, it was a life-changing period of transition, moving on to play for Darlington and Aberdeen before heading over to Denmark for spells with Silkeborg IF and OB...

My first goalkeeping hero wasn't British. Before the greatness of Peter Shilton and Neville Southall made its impression, the spectacular and often flamboyant style of Bruce Grobbelaar grabbed my attention. He made goalkeeping appear exciting, and British goalkeepers dull in comparison.

Keepers such as Joel Bats, Luis Arconada, Hans van Breukelen and and Rinat Dasayev all emanated a mystique that lured me towards them, exuding confidence and belief. A positive arrogance and pride in their position. My adolescent view of British goalkeepers was that they were too humble in the way they went about their jobs, almost apologetically so.

Our myopic sense that we produced the best keepers in the world ignored the heritage of Russia, Germany and Italy, and once the Premier League opened its doors to the rest of Europe, the influx of keepers from the continent became a flood.

The greatest import of them all, Peter Schmeichel, began his dominance in the field and suddenly the DNA of goalkeeping in this country was changed forever. Quite literally 'foreign' techniques, once so derided, were shown to be an asset in the modern game. Skills founded in handball, futsal and basketball extended beyond the rigidity of our own.

Punching and parrying were on their way to becoming acceptable rather than seen as over-cautious or indecisive, and only in recent years has resistance been broken to doing away with certain traditional, previously unquestioned techniques. The result? Keepers that can challenge our counterparts in the rest of the world as equals once more.

As a kid at Sunderland it might have seemed a case of turkeys voting for Christmas, but I welcomed the arrivals from abroad. I'd held a dream of playing in France since becoming obsessed with their side of '84 to '86.

I fulfilled the dream of playing abroad, albeit in Denmark, another of the nations to light up Mexico '86. The contrast in coaching was huge, with far more attention given to technical detail than hard work and repetitive up/down drills that I'd been brought up on.

I was able to look through the window into German and Dutch football and see for myself why we had been left behind.

AUTOGLASS

UMBRO

UNFORGETTABLES

MART POOM

The Greatest SAVES No 2

LEV YASHIN
CCCP 1-2 WEST GERMANY
Date: 25 July 1966
Venue: Goodison Park

In the semi-final of the 1966 World Cup, the well-drilled West Germans showed too much class for the combative Russians. There was just one position where the Soviets held an obvious superiority – between the posts, where the legendary Lev Yashin was playing his last part in a major tournament.

An acknowledged world star, the Black Spider exuded a calm and stately presence in his all-black kit, while his grubby knee bandage signalled a oneness with the proletariat. You can dial up the match on YouTube and watch the tall figure spring into life to save a 35-yard thunderbolt from the insolent Lothar Emmerich.

"The joy of seeing Yuri Gagarin flying in space," Yashin once commented, "is only superseded by the joy of a good penalty save."

We can only echo those words of wisdom, adding that the sight of the master arcing majestically through the Liverpool air also figures right up there among life's affordable pleasures.

Like a black spider...

MANAGER GOALIES

Arguably, the goalkeeper has the sharpest possible perspective on the two most important aspects of the game of football. They know every offensive trick in the book – and are perfectly drilled on how to counter every one. In addition, the goalkeeper is often the loudest voice on the pitch, the inspirational guardian of team spirit as well as the lobster pot. So how come so few goalies go on to become top managers when they hang up their gloves?

Is there perhaps a feeling that the specialist keeper is unqualified to motivate and organise outfield players? There surely can't be doubts about shouldering responsibility.

The fact that only two ex-custodians have managed Premier League clubs begins to feel a little like a conspiracy. Mike Walker was relieved of his duties at Everton back in 1994, leaving Southampton's Nigel Adkins as the only modern boss to have made the transition. With all due respect to the former Watford/Colchester and Tranmere/Wigan keepers, isn't it slightly odd that none of the higher-profile goalies have had a go at managing in the PL era?

Looking further back, the likes of Peter Shilton and Ray Clemence at least tried and failed at lowly Plymouth and Barnet; but it was usually lesser-known goalies (Jock Wallace, Berwick Rangers; Don Mackay, Dundee United) who later popped up wearing flared suits on the touchline.

We're left looking abroad for goalkeepers who have successfully made the move into the manager's office. Dino Zoff is a notable exception to the rule, a 1982 World Cup winner who then came close to bossing Italy to Euro 2000 triumph. Belgian international goalie Raymond Goethals coached Marseille to victory over Milan in the 1993 Champions League final. The current Russian coach, Stanislav Cherchesov, is a former international goalie. On the home front, the best we can do is Walter Zenga getting sacked

Dynasty: Mike Walker, father of Ian.

JOCK WALLACE (Manager) / RANGERS

after three months at Wolves.

At least, in Peter Taylor, goaliedom can claim the most influential assistant manager of the 20th century!

FIRST GLOVE

David James
"My first pair were the Sondico League Specials similar to the ones Ray Clemence wore, but the cheaper version with embossed rubber grip and in red polyurethane."

TABLE TOP KEEPERS - PART 1

Your tireless authors spent an afternoon road-testing some familiar old table/carpet level favourites from the keeper's point of view. It's a tough job, but somebody has to do it…

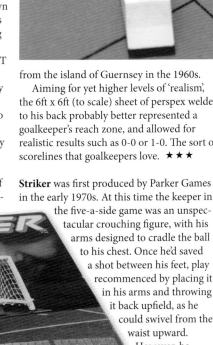

Subbuteo had a wide range of accessories which extended to their goalkeeping options. You could have crouching keepers, diving goalkeepers, diving goalkeepers wearing caps, 'live action' keepers (wobbling on a spring), and keepers taking a goal kick. They allowed for a certain level of skill, aided by the fact that they were saving a ball as tall as themselves. But, with them not being anchored down to anything, a particularly vigorous dive could see them uprooting the entire goal frame and netting. Shouting: "WHAT A SAVE!", when your goal has ended up halfway between the six-yard box and the corner flag, can lead to a heated exchange with an opponent who values the rule book above the sheer joy of the game. ★ ★ ★ ★

T.A.F. 4-2-4 was a more scientific version of Subbuteo, painstakingly created by Tom Waterman, a signwriter from the island of Guernsey in the 1960s.

Aiming for yet higher levels of 'realism', the 6ft x 6ft (to scale) sheet of perspex welded to his back probably better represented a goalkeeper's reach zone, and allowed for realistic results such as 0-0 or 1-0. The sort of scorelines that goalkeepers love. ★ ★ ★

Striker was first produced by Parker Games in the early 1970s. At this time the keeper in the five-a-side game was an unspectacular crouching figure, with his arms designed to cradle the ball to his chest. Once he'd saved a shot between his feet, play recommenced by placing it in his arms and throwing it back upfield, as he could swivel from the waist upward. However, he would often forget to let go in time and sling the ball

round into his
own net. Gary Sprake did this once for Leeds at Anfield, but the Striker goalie could do it three or four times per game.

Then came the diving goalkeeper, a lovely piece of engineering, whose arms stretched out as you moved him to the side with a very pleasing motion.

The chances of you being able to react in time to tip a fierce shot round the post were minimal, however. ★★/★★★★★

Casdon Soccer was good bashabout fun, with its sturdy moulded plastic pitch, though the goalkeeper was no design classic. Once

you'd inevitably
mislaid the little keeper
figure that slotted on top of the bat,
you were left with a rotating slab, like a
bucking bronco machine that had thrown its rider.

There was nothing this keeper could do about a well-placed shot just inside the post, but if you managed to middle the ball bearing on the sweet spot your opponent was in danger of losing a front tooth. ★★

LOOKING AFTER NUMBER 1

Goalie Endorsements

No 2 - Ray Clemence

Knice Keeping Ray Klemence
from **Knorr**®

As the greatest goalie of his generation (even if he was the equal best, it still counts in marketing), Ray Clemence had his pick of all the toppermost of the notchernost products to put his name to back in the halcyon days of 70s advertising.

Sporting gear, groceries, grooming products. The advertisers were queuing up at Ray's door

Ray Clemence also plays Badminton & Squash to a high standard

...using **SunBatta** rackets & accessories

SUN BATTA (UK) LTD.
Ross Place, Liverpool L3 3BN Telephone: 051 207 2560

for endorsements – though seemingly many brands weren't particularly interested by the top shot-stopper's key attributes.

Back in the 50s and early 60s, those sorry old black-and-

No drink can beat it. Milk is supreme.

white days just after the war, keepers were regularly called upon to feature in adverts for banks and building societies. Save with the Leicester Permanent. Geddit? Cunningly, these wily financial institutions would employ semi-successful line drawings of goalkeepers at full stretch in order to cling on to their own precious pennies.

But in the easy-going anarchy of the late 70s, Ray strode free from the need for any such literal references. He was free to endorse whatever he liked. There was no 'catch' involved. No need for a savings bank 'punch'-line. This was the dawning of the age of celebrity.

True, Ray did have to successfully hold up several packets of soup whilst having a hard 'c' sound at the start of his surname, but you didn't have to be the England goalie to tick those boxes.

40

He also had to pose with a bottle of milk at the same time as taking off his goalie jersey – a big ask – but again Ray proved equal to the task.

Perhaps most randomly of all, the Clemence stamp of approval was applied to badminton equipment and Geest bananas.

"Ray Clemence is going great bananas," went the catchphrase on everybody's lips back in 1977. To which the correct witty response was: "I beg your pardon?"

Lenthéric hair products and Ray Clemence, England goalkeeper, had a natural mutual affinity. We're guessing it was a suitably weedy pun on 'Barnet', where Ray would experiment with management in the 1990s, before joining the England set-up as goalkeeping coach. Strangely, Ray's hair looked much better in the Knorr soup advert than in the plug for sexy grooming aids, but maybe we

shouldn't read too much into that fact.

Sadly, Ray's advertising sub-career came to an abrupt end when he broke the bit-part's golden rule: never work with children or animals. From this point on, every time Umbro or anyone else needed a winning smile in a Liverpool tracksuit, they were straight on the blower to his daughter, Sarah.

DROP KICK G

CHARLIE
WILLIAMS

1900
MAN CITY v SUNDERLAND

PAT
JENNINGS

1967
SPURS v MANCHESTER UTD

P
SH

LEICESTER v

STEVE
OGRIZOVIC

1986
COVENTRY v SHEFFIELD WED

ANDY
LONERGAN

2004
PRESTON NORTH END v LEICESTER

A
MA

MANSFIELD TO

OALSCORERS

SEAMUS
McDONAGH

1983
BOLTON WANDERERS v BURNLEY

STEVE
SHERWOOD

1984
WATFORD v COVENTRY

PTON

GARETH
WILLIAMS

2016
TRETHOMAS BLUEBIRDS v CAERLEON

JAMIE
BUTLER

2016
HEMEL HEMPSTEAD TOWN v SUTTON UTD

EXHAM

KIDS IN KITS

It was a magic feeling, pulling on your team's goalie shirt, shorts and socks. And then looking down at the badge. It was the kind of occasion that warranted pestering your mother to get the camera out.

"Mam, take it now. Take it while I'm doing this..."

Waiting impatiently between shots while she 'wound it on'. Crouching with your Wembley Trophy football clutched safely in your arms – or maybe you'd try an action shot, diving dangerously close to the rose bushes for a ball lobbed gently in the air...

At that moment, it wasn't your mam any more, it was the official club photographer on photocall day, taking the photo that would appear in *Shoot!* or on a football card. Or else you were your club's brand new signing, and a gaggle of snappers from the dailies was eagerly crowded round you.

"I think I've come to the end of the film," says Mam as her winder-onner meets resistance.

"Take it anyway!" you implore from mid-air, reaching out to touch the shot around the blur of an imaginary upright. The one that got away.

44

Above left: the 70s perfectly captured in a single photo.

SECRET GOALIES

Here's a whole team made up of goalies who were more famous in another guise. Uniquely, it's a side where every player wears a number 1 on their back, lining up in a distinctly defensive 0-0-0 formation...

Banksy

No, not Gordon Banks but rather England's number one guerrilla spray artist. Not a lot of people know that Britain's most famous anonymous artist used to play for a Bristol amateur team, the Easton Cowboys. In 2001 he joined his team-mates on a tour of Mexico, lining up against a team made up of local freedom fighters.

Che Guevara

And, following up on the South American revolutionary theme, it's cool to learn that Argentine freedom-fighter and poster boy Che Guevara was also a Secret Goalie. Well, he does always seem to be associated with green shirts.

Sir David Frost

In his teenage years the great TV interrogator played for Nottingham Forest's Youth team before he was whisked away to Cambridge University. Frost was a gifted cricketer as well as an excellent goalkeeper, show-ing enough promise to be offered a contract by Forest. At university, he went on to appear between the sticks for his college, starring for the Gonville & Caius AFC 1st XI of 1958/59.

Albert Camus

The author of the existential-ist classic *The Outsider*, Camus gained his philo-sophical grounding in goals

for the Racing Universitaire Algerios (RUA) junior team, before TB intervened.

David Icke

Injury forced former Coventry and Hereford keeper David Icke to retire from football at the age of 21, when he reinvented himself as a local sports reporter and then BBC sports presenter on *Grandstand*. It was after he became a spokesperson for the Green Party that Dave alerted the world to a grand conspiracy by shape-shifting reptilian extra-terrestrials who aim to suppress humanity by tampering with our DNA to prevent us from harnessing the full potential of our brains.

Niels Bohr

Bohr was a Danish physicist who received the Nobel Prize for Physics in 1922 for his work in quantum mechanics. Even playing in goals for the Akademisk Boldklub at the University of Copenhagen, he continued his work on the fundamental laws of physics. For every incoming shot, he worked out the lift forces on a 410-450g sphere (around 3.5 Newtons) versus the velocity of the ball (25-30 metres per second), its acceleration (8 metres per second per second) and spin (8-10 revolutions per second) – not forgetting the variable viscosity of the air and its flow over the surface of the ball. Simple.

Sir Arthur Conan Doyle

It's often reported that the creator of Sherlock Holmes was Portsmouth's goalie in the Victorian era. However, his football career ended in 1896, and

Conan the Custodian.

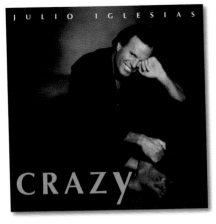

Pompey were not founded until 1898. Therefore, we can deduce it was actually the amateur side Portsmouth AFC that Conan Doyle played for – under the pseudonym A.C. Smith.

Julio Iglesias

Perma-tanned crooner Julio Iglesias was on Real Madrid's books in the early 60s, balancing his duties as a law student with those of a Secret Goalie. Sadly, he was involved in a car accident in 1963 which resulted in an injury to his spinal cord and the end of his potential football career. It was Julio's car crash which led to him take up the guitar during his convalescence, resulting in the sale of some 300 million records.

Dr James Spensley

Virtually unknown in his native UK, Spensley has an Italian park, a street and a junior football tournament named in his honour. According to Keith Baker's excellent *Fathers Of Football*, Spensley's great contribution to Italian football was "persuading the British expat Genoa Cricket and Athletic Club to take up the association game. Spensley became the club's goalkeeper, captain and manager, leading Genoa to six Italian championships between 1898 and 1904. Their success saw the club renamed the Genoa Cricket and Football Club – a name they retain today."

Felix Mourinho

There's only one man in football likely to have topped the insane self-regard of José 'The Special One' Mourinho – and that's his father and role model. While José is a rare

example of a manager who never played the game professionally, his father Felix enjoyed a long career with Belenenses and Vitória Setúbal, winning a solitary cap for Portugal in 1972.

Nicky Byrne

The Westlife singer-songwriter was a member of Leeds United's 1997 FA Youth Cup winning squad. The clues are all over Byrne's output. Westlife's second single was a paranoid ode to the threat of the tricky looping cross, entitled 'If I Let You Go'. He managed to salt lingering memories and obsessions from his goalkeeping days into teenybop smashes 'Seasons in the Sun', 'Flying Without Wings' and 'Ain't That a Kick in the Head?'.

FIRST GLOVE

Bryan Gunn

"Hamish Morrison at Ross County gave me my first proper pair of gloves, which were the Uhlsport 037s in yellow and black. I loved them, they were brilliant."

The Greatest SAVES

No 3

DAVID SEAMAN
ARSENAL 1-0 SHEFFIELD UTD
Date: 13 April 2003
Venue: Old Trafford

Goalkeepers are often superstitious souls, putting their faith in the alignment of the planets as much as that of the defensive wall. Even before the match, the 2003 FA Cup semi-final between Arsenal and Sheffield United at Old Trafford seemed fraught with significance. Arsenal keeper David Seaman was making his 1,000th senior appearance.

But the fateful nature of this pivotal day was to keep on growing.

"I was fortunate enough to make one or two important saves from penalties for England," Seaman later reflected. "But from open play that one at Old Trafford was probably the best."

In the 84th minute, with Arsenal 1-0 up, a loose ball from a corner looped dramatically to Paul Peschisolido, three yards out. He nodded it goalwards but Seaman somehow produced a backwards dive, clawing the ball away from right above the line.

As a direct result of the wonder save, Arsenal made it to the FA Cup final. Seaman was captain for the day, and lifted the trophy. "Although I didn't know it at the time, it turned out to be my last game for Arsenal. I went to Manchester City in the summer but six months later I had to retire because of a shoulder injury."

Unbelievable...

VIDEO NICETIES

Do you remember videocassette recorders? The VCR seemed like magic when TV-taping technology first appeared in the 70s. It gave you the chance to watch *Match of the Day* at absolutely any time you wanted, not just at 10 o'clock on a Saturday night, when Jimmy Hill had previously exerted a spooky ability to empty busy pubs.

And what about the videocassette itself? If you're too young for any of this to make sense, they were a bit like a long plastic ribbon spooling from reel to reel in a little black box, spilling TV pics as they spun.

Nowadays, the technology admittedly sounds a bit rusty. Videos are so far past their sell-by date, most charity shops have actually banned their donation. But back in the days before YouTube there was no better way to savour a goalkeeping bonanza in the privacy of your own front room (and kit and gloves, to help build the mood!)

Goalie vids came in three types: the coaching video, the documentary/biography, and the super-successful saves compilation. "So You Want to be a Goal-keeper?" Bryan Gunn asks,

Videos: taking up valuable garage space since 2001.

make my day.'"

Personally, it would make our day if anyone could explain why there were only 109 rather than the standard 110 Second Division Saves of the Season in 91-92.

before coming over all Clint Eastwood: "With the right coaching you too can have the confidence that says, 'Just try it –

"Red sauce, brown sauce, or no sauce at all?"
"Mustard."

DEPUTY KEEPERS

"He also serves, who only stands and waits..." but sometimes he has to get his kit on, pronto.

In the days before the substitutes bench extended to the point where goalkeepers were included, there could be all manner of shenanigans if the No 1 got injured. If this happened during the match then we were able to enjoy the high entertainment of an outfield player going in goal, though this was unfair on the second choice keeper who could spend months or even years waiting for his turn. Only a pre-match warm-up injury would mean that the deputy keeper could step in at short notice.

They appeared in the team group photos, played for the reserves, and watched first-team games from the stands, secretly hoping that the bloke stubbornly occupying the number one shirt would crock himself during the kick-in.

This is what happened one Sunday at Filbert Street in September 1992. On the occasion of Leicester City's first live televised League game, versus Wolves, Carl Muggleton pulled a muscle in his back a few minutes

before kick-off.

City's other first team keeper Kevin Poole was out with an injury, so a search party was sent up to the Main Stand to locate the whereabouts of Youth-team custodian Russell Hoult. He was found tucking into a pre-match hot dog, and informed that he was about to make his League debut.

Russell performed very well, keeping a clean sheet against Wolves' prolific strike partnership of Steve Bull and Andy Mutch in a 0-0 draw. Although he had to endure a post-match microphone-up-the-nose interview from Central TV's Gary Newbon, he got to take home a bottle of Barclays Man of the Match bubbly, and also a power drill from the electrical company who sponsored the game. Any mention of him in Leicester will still elicit the response: "Ahh, the Hot Dog Kid!"

Perhaps the most famous of the stand-in keepers was Nigel Spink who was suddenly thrust into a European Cup Final in 1982. Aston Villa were the firm underdogs when they a faced a Bayern Munich side boasting the likes of Paul Breitner and Karl-Heinz Rummenigge, in Amsterdam. And there was a major setback in the 9th minute when Jimmy Rimmer had to concede that a neck injury picked up in training was still troubling him, despite the painkillers.

At least, it would have been a setback, if Spink hadn't performed so brilliantly in only his second first-team game for Villa (his debut being two and a half years previously). Spink and his defence kept wave after wave of Bayern attacks at bay before Peter Withe popped up with a winner.

Spink had benefitted from the larger number of subs allowed in European ties, but in the domestic game the only solution to an injured keeper was to stick one of his outfield team-mates between the sticks. This was a fairly common occurence, so much so that you can make a full side out of England international players who stood in for their keepers in club games: Bobby Moore, John Terry, Phil Jagielka, Rio Ferdinand, Glenn Hoddle, David Platt, Graham Roberts, John Salako, Peter Beardsley, Peter Withe, Harry Kane. Sub: Neil Webb.

The stand-in keeper has had varying degrees of success. Bobby Moore saved a penalty for West Ham against Stoke, but was then gutted when Mike Bernard hammered in the rebound. Niall Quinn also saved a spot-kick for Manchester City versus Derby having just replaced the red-carded Tony Coton. (Quinn was a fairly competent keeper and was the Republic of Ireland's third choice for Italia 90, as Jack Charlton only named Pat Bonner and Gerry Peyton.)

But Harry Kane had a brief stint in goal to forget. Having scored his first hat-trick for Tottenham in a Europa Cup tie against Asteras Tripoli, Kane pulled on Hugo Lloris's shirt after the keeper's late dismissal. Kane's first touch saw him allow a tame free-kick to squirm through his grasp. As this made the score 5-1, the Spurs fans could afford to laugh about it.

Leicester's Alan Young stood in for Mark Wallington after Shrewsbury's Chic Bates had put a stud hole in his thigh in an FA Cup quarter-final in 1982. But Young was then

One of Glen Hoddle's THREE turns in goal.

UNFORGETTABLES

NIGEL SPINK

knocked out and in turn had to be replaced by winger Steve Lynex. He later regained his senses, and the green shirt.

It's a shame that this crowd pleasing possibility is ever more remote with the introduction of seven substitutes.

No longer can real keepers say: "See? it's not as easy as it looks."

FIRST GLOVE

Alan Knight

"My first proper ones, after the green cotton gloves, were a pair of Adidas Curkovic which I got from a sports shop close to where I used to live in Streatham. Peter Mellor also got hold of some Gola gloves around this time too which were similar, but not as good."

wore a pair in the 1922 FA Cup Final. While most preferred to play bare-handed, successive generations of goalkeepers continued to use these repurposed gloves on occasion, with all their attendant flaws (a lack of grip and tendency to absorb water being the main offenders).

There is, of course, a difference between these gloves worn by goalkeepers, and gloves developed specifically for goalkeeping. It wasn't until the early 60s that some keepers began experimenting with gloves enhanced by pimpled rubber from table tennis bats sewn into the fingers and palms. Gordon Banks made his famous save from Pele's header in such a pair, in the hot and dusty conditions in Mexico City. But what we think of as the modern goalkeeper glove, worn today by every professional and grassroots keeper around the world, began with West German goalkeeper Sepp Maier.

Gebhard Reusch, son of Reusch founder Karl, worked closely with Maier to produce gloves with a latex foam palm. Latex was immediately superior to pimpled rubber because it was softer, more flexible and offered better grip and shock absorption. Despite these advantages, many leading goalkeepers finished the 1970s still wearing the pimpled rubber gloves, or playing bare-handed. It wasn't until Reusch and fellow German innovators Uhlsport began mass-producing latex-palmed gloves that goalkeepers at every level caught on. In some cases, this happened purely from those in the 'Goalkeeper's Union' wanting to help out their brethren. QPR goalkeeper Phil Parkes was given a pair to try by German keeper Wolfgang Kleff during a pre-season friendly and Dave Sexton, QPR manager at the time, kept him in stock via his German contacts. Parkes proudly showed them off to Brian Moore on *The Big Match* in 1975.

While the advantages of latex gloves

GLOVE EVOLUTION

The evolution of the goalkeeper glove was complicated by the fact that for many decades, goalkeepers regularly wore gloves that were not designed for them at all. Simple woollen or cotton gardening gloves were utilised as far back as the 1800s, usually (but not always) in cold or wet conditions.

Scottish goalkeeper Archie Pinnell was photographed wearing a pair of gloves in the mid 1890s, and Preston North End's James Mitchell

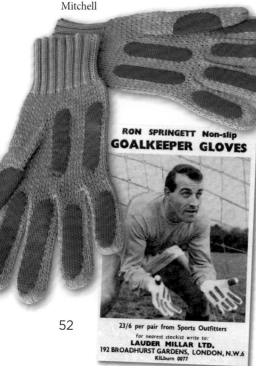

RON SPRINGETT Non-slip
GOALKEEPER GLOVES

23/6 per pair from Sports Outfitters
for nearest stockist write to:
LAUDER MILLAR LTD.
192 BROADHURST GARDENS, LONDON, N.W.6
KILburn 0077

became immediately apparent to the early adopters, one drawback quickly became clear: they didn't last very long. Every keeper who played with early versions recalls large chunks coming off the fingertips, sometimes with the very first usage. But as glove technology advanced, latex palms improved in both grip and durability. Today, latex palms will flake and wear gradually, and a properly cared-for glove can last an entire season.

Major innovations in recent decades include Adidas's introduction of 'Fingersave' gloves, latex designed specifically for wet weather, and the development of new palm cuts and styles of gloves.

Reusch developed the first roll finger cut, which encased the finger completely in latex without side gussets. This style has remained popular, while cuts such as negative (with the gusset seam stitching hidden inside the glove,

for a tighter fit) and hybrid cuts offer today's goalkeepers an array of options that the likes of Banks, Bonetti, and even Sepp Maier could only have dreamt of.

SONDICO HORNE PRO
£26.99

UHL 092
£28.95

SONDICO SOLAR
£28.99

UHL 025
£30.95

UHL 083
£30.95

SONDICO PRO FILE
£31.99

REUSCH MINI
£31.99

UHL 071
£33.45

REUSCH ANDREWS
£33.99

REUSCH SEAMAN
£35.99

UHL 036
£38.95

reusch
Torwarthandschuhe
Hans van Breukelen

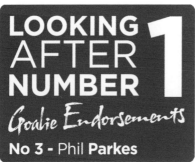

LOOKING AFTER NUMBER 1

Goalie Endorsements

No 3 - Phil **Parkes**

Ask any defensive, pre-blokey teenager of the late 70s to squirt his barnet with hairspray and his response would probably fail to pass any one of a hundred modern-day safeguards designed to foster equal rights

and to outlaw gender assumptions. To roughly paraphrase, hairspray was for ladies.

However, ask the same spotty herbert if he fancied an hour and a half rolling in mud with 20 other men before diving all together into a steamy team bath... heck, that was about as manly as you could get.

In order to bridge the metrosexual divide 30 years before the term was dreamed up, Cossack cleverly employed QPR and England goalie Phil Parkes. Phil only resorted to 'hair control' because he had "just finished an hour and a half of diving, scrambling, lunging and kicking a football away from his muddy goal."

In the 70s, blokes' hairspray was always carefully named after martial arts or militaristic tribes. Rest assured, one squib of 'greasy hair formula' swordsman's sex glue on your coiffure and you'd quite literally be knocking the ladies dead.

SHILTS AND CLEM

Shilton or Clemence – which was the better keeper? Was it burly, in-your-face, super-fit shot-stopper 'Tarzan' or the more slender, laid-back, quick-off-the-line sweeper keeper 'Clem'? Throughout the 70s and 80s the debate raged, with experts doing their best to compare the pair's very different styles and their almost identically excellent results for club and country. Ramsey favoured Shilton. Mercer and Revie favoured Clemence, to the extent that Shilton withdrew from the international scene. Temporarily.

The two men, who were rivals for the title of world's best keeper – the best of friends off the field, eternal England roommates and training partners – would be forever bound together as an inseparable pair.

Looking back on the England set-up of the era, it was the supreme affability of England boss Ron Greenwood that led to one of the strangest selection decisions in goalkeeping history. Big Ron decided to make no decision. Instead, he opted to alternate the pair in the hope that one would eventually emerge as top dog.

And so the odd couple continued, inseparable in every way. The pair even recorded a terrible pub singalong single together, 'Side by Side'. They both wrote for football magazines, Clemence for *Shoot!* and Shilton for *Top Soccer*, moving to the former when the titles merged. Both endorsed Sondico sports gloves. And throughout their careers, magazines churned out the annual feature 'Who is England's Number 1?'. It's up to you to choose...

Did You Know?: The final score was Shilton 125-61 Clemence.

SIDE by SIDE
PETER and RAY
SHILTON CLEMENCE

55

REUSCH

There are many different versions of the genesis of goalkeeper gloves, but no company stakes a more credible claim as originators of the modern, latex-based glove than Reusch.

The company, formed in 1934 and specialising in gloves for alpine sports as well as football, worked with German World Cup winner Sepp Maier to mass produce versions of his over-sized latex gloves. Although it took some time for distributors and retailers to help make the gloves readily available, they proved one of the greatest hits in football's retail history. Every goalkeeper at the 1982 World Cup wore latex-palm goalkeeper gloves, and no keeper since has failed to do so. They are as much a staple of the game as shin pads and boots.

It wasn't always so. Before the innovation of latex gloves, goalkeepers were limited to either their bare hands, or, on wet or cold days, cotton and wool gloves that were occasionally enhanced with strips of rubber from table tennis bats. With Reusch at the vanguard, latex represented a leap forward in performance that hasn't been matched since.

In the 1980s, Reusch often personalised models for the pros who wore them, adding their initials to the backhand design, and the company was quick to adapt to the decade's new colour palettes, introducing models with neon green, pink and purple featuring prominently. It's one thing to be an innovator but quite another to establish a permanent presence in the game at both the highest professional and grassroots levels.

Reusch has never wanted for professional endorsement. At the 1996 Euros, almost every goal-

56

keeper wore the company's now-iconic World Keeper model, featuring their much-beloved (and now sadly missed) arrow logo.

Reusch gloves have lifted no fewer than five World Cup trophies. Among the company's many famous pros, perhaps none were valued so highly as Manchester United's Peter Schmeichel, who hoisted the Champions League trophy in 1999 in his signature 'S' model gloves.

It's an image at once enduring and emblematic of the Reusch brand.

International Choice...

A SECRET WHY NEARLY ALL THE TOP
S AROUND THE WORLD RELY ON
GOALKEEPER GLOVES...IT'S THEIR
SUPER GRIPPING POWER!

KEEPERS OF THE SILVER SCREEN

Ask any football fan – or any film fan for that matter – about their favourite soccer movie, and the chances are the flick they pick will come from a pool of just three, all of which feature a major goalkeeping sub-plot.

The arty film student will probably want to namecheck *The Goalkeeper's Fear of the Penalty*, a 1972 German drama directed by Wim Wenders. Despite the title, the film is less concerned with the titular goalie's pre-match preparations than the murder he commits after getting sent off for dissent. It takes the concept of goalkeepers being slightly barking to a whole new level, which even the masterful John Burridge couldn't compete with!

Everyone who grew up in the 80s has a soft spot for *Gregory's Girl*, a Scottish teenage rom-com that revolves around a school team's new star player – a girl, for heaven's sake! – who takes the hapless Gregory's place up front. So he's forced to try and prove his worth in goals. If you were a FRANKIE SAYS T-shirt type, or Radio 1 DJ John Peel, the high point of the film was surely Gregory's date with Clare Grogan of Altered Images, who ultimately turns out to be 'his girl'.

From a goalie's perspective, however, the highlight is undoubtedly the iconic yellow keeper gloves – complete with green pimpled padding – that Gregory wears during his disastrous debut between the sticks. We can also guarantee you a minor extra thrill the next time you see the film, by revealing (some 37 years after *Shoot!*) that "Dee and

Gordon were taught some of the basic skills by Partick Thistle and Scotland keeper Alan Rough."

Lastly, there's *Escape to Victory*. As one correspondent to *Metro* once commented, it's the greatest war movie ever made about football. However, the only other vaguely comparable film is the obscure American movie *The Boys From Company C*, which was set during the Vietnam conflict and features a team of grunts who refuse to lose to a local Army side in return for their tickets home. Not a blockbuster.

The appeal of *Escape to Victory* lies in the inspired casting. Michael Caine – the film world's equivalent of Bobby Moore in the 1960s – lining up next to Bobby Moore, the, er, footballing equivalent of Michael Caine. Add into the mix Ossie Ardiles, John Wark, Russell Osman and Pele, and director John Huston clearly had a winner on his hands. But it was the decision to put Sylvester Stallone in goal that really swung it for many. When it was first released, the British public howled in derision at the thought. An American? In goal? It was arguably a greater fantasy adventure than *The Never Ending Story*.

That was until the 1990s, when a certain Kasey Keller appeared on the scene at Millwall, closely followed by the likes of Tim Howard and Brad Friedel. Suddenly having a Yank in goal saving a German penalty wasn't so bonkers after all.

Of course, there have been other goalie-related movies. Of them all, an honourable mention must go to *Kes*, thanks to Dai Bradley's performance as Billy Casper, the ultimate unwilling schoolboy keeper – even though his attempt to steal the football scene by swinging from the crossbar was overshadowed by Brian Glover pretending to be Bobby Charlton in midfield.

And so to the many real-life goalkeepers who have tested out their acting abilities in front of the camera – alas, a thespian masterclass that will have to wait until *Glove Story 2*...

JIM MONTGOMERY
SUNDERLAND 1-0 LEEDS UNITED
Date: 5 May 1973
Venue: Wembley Stadium
At the 1973 FA Cup final, hot favourites Leeds United found themselves 1-0 down

to the Mackems, and began to pile on the pressure.

"The high one in!" BBC commentator David Coleman yelped. "And Cherry going in!! And a great save!!! And a goal!!!! No!!!!! My goodness, I thought Lorimer had got that one."

Trevor Cherry had forced a diving header goalward, which Jim Montgomery could only parry away to the feet of Peter Lorimer, who blasted the bobbling ball into the empty net. But somehow, diving the wrong way into his own goal, Monty appeared out of nowhere to deflect the ball up on to the bar.

Impossible.

And a goal... No!...

Лев Яшин (Динамо Москва)

GOALKEEPERS NAMECHECKED BY HALF MAN HALF BISCUIT

Goalkeeper	Song
Luis Arconada	Emerging from Gorse
Joel Bats	Emerging from Gorse
Joseph-Antoine Bell	Emerging from Gorse
George Farm	1966 and All That
Brad Friedel	I Went to a Wedding...
Peter Grummitt	Let's Not
Jean-Marie Pfaff	Emerging from Gorse
Mart Poom	Left Lyrics in the Practice Room
Bob Wilson	Bob Wilson, Anchorman

HALF · MAN · HALF · BISCUIT
side 2
PROBE PLUS
333 rpm
PROBE 4

WHAT'S THE POINT?

Never mind all those hours spent in the nets stopping shots, or those hard-learned lessons about positioning and communication. All that technical stuff is fine in theory, but out in the confusion of the frontline (aka the backline) it's all secondary to the goalkeeper's most vital skill. Pointing.

Oh yes, and shouting. Pointing and shouting. That's the way forward in most goalkeeping scenarios. You'll do well to make it your default state.

Example 1: A defender lets an attacker get a shot in. What is your correct response? To sprint from your line, pointing and shouting, gesturing at your team-mates to close down, to concentrate, to use their eyes. Shots at goal can make things awkward for you, so best give them a wake-up clap, too.

Example 2: You make a decent save. After the chest bumps and high fives have subsided, stride out into your area and do some pointless pointing to hide your blushes.

Example 3: Ideally, you'd like everybody to think you are in control of your area at a corner or free-kick. Point and shout at your defensive wall. At the oppo pushing and shoving. At your girlfriend who seems to be talking to one of their subs on the touchline.

David Harvey
points the way
to the top of the
mountain at
Elland Road.

Legends on the line No 3 Gordon Banks

It was a thrill and an honour to meet up with the great Gordon Banks of Leicester City, Stoke City and England, near to his home in the Potteries...

First things first, could we take you back to 1959, when you first appeared on most football fans' radar?

"I'll try. When you get to my age, your memory's not so clever, and that was over 50 years ago. I'd played professionally for around half a season in the Third Division when the Chesterfield manager had me in and told me they'd had an offer from Leicester, which they had accepted – and would I be interested in going? I said yes, thank you, straight away. It was a big

GORDON BANKS

Goalkeeper
STOKE CITY

opportunity to go and play in the top league."

Were you nervous when you quickly got the chance to step up from the reserves?

"Well, yes. Pre-match nerves were there every time you played. Especially when you're sitting in the dressing room and just about to go out. Even when you're shooting in. But as soon as the whistle went you had to push all that behind you and concentrate on your game."

What was goalkeeper training like back in the early 60s?

"There was none of the specialist goalkeeper training then. I had to do the outfield training, run the laps, do all the exercises, and then we'd finish up with five-a-side. But because we didn't have an actual training ground then, we had to play on the Filbert Street car park. I couldn't dive about on that surface so I didn't go in goal, I played outfield. A few years later, when they got the training ground, that gave me the opportunity to go back in the afternoon. The lads finished training at lunchtime, so I had to get some of the apprentices and reserves to come back in the afternoon and bang some balls at me."

Goalkeeping experts always talk about your positional sense. Was that something that came naturally to you, or did you have to work on it?

"You have to work on it to get it to the highest level. Those long afternoons helped me quite a lot. But just as important was all those many hours spent playing as a boy, maybe playing with a tennis ball or whatever. Even if you were playing against an old shed, you'd still be learning where to stand in a given situation. You didn't realise at the time you were learning about angles."

After two FA Cup finals and winning the League Cup with Leicester, you got your first England call-up.

"I was down at the ground when I found out about it. Matt Gillies, the manager, came into our snooker room, shook me by the hand and said, 'Congratulations, you're in the England team.' I couldn't quite believe it as the squad hadn't even assembled yet. Obviously, Alf must have said something to him. It was something of a shock and a great delight. I remember feeling very, very proud."

Your international debut was against Scotland at Wembley. A nice easy one to start with?

"Oh crikey, not half! Every single time we played Scotland over the years, no matter whether at Wembley or Hampden, it was a really tough game. About 90 per cent of the Scots played in the English First Division so

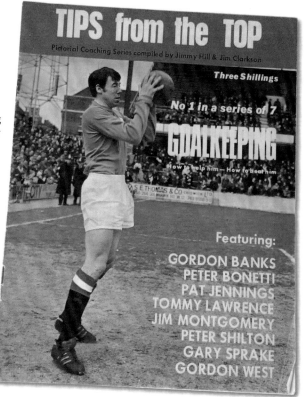

TIPS from the TOP

Pictorial Coaching Series compiled by Jimmy Hill & Jim Clarkson

Three Shillings

No 1 in a series of 7

GOALKEEPING

How to help him — How to beat him

Featuring:

GORDON BANKS
PETER BONETTI
PAT JENNINGS
TOMMY LAWRENCE
JIM MONTGOMERY
PETER SHILTON
GARY SPRAKE
GORDON WEST

they were always a match for us. We lost 2-1. They got a penalty past me, and I was feeling quite down, but Alf Ramsey came up to me and said, 'Well played.' That gave me a bit of a lift and I was pleased that he'd seen something in my game."

Do you still get asked about 1966 every day of your life?

"What can you say that would describe how it feels to win the World Cup? It was a fantastic feeling. I knew I had lots of years left in the game, as I'd trained well and worked hard, so at the time I didn't see it as the pinnacle of my career. I thought that both England and Leicester City would push on from there and get better. Both were good set-ups with players coming to the best part of their careers. I thought really that was just the beginning."

But that season after the World Cup was your last at Leicester.

"I'd seen Peter Shilton occasionally while he was playing for Leicester City Boys and

then he got in the England Schoolboys side. I saw him in the gym – two mats down, with trainer George Dewis banging balls at him. I watched him for five minutes and I thought, bloody hell, this lad has got some real technique here!

When he signed as an apprentice, he'd join in on the little goalkeeping sessions that I organised."

How did you feel when you were transferlisted?

"I was shocked and amazed. I couldn't believe that they'd want to get rid of me. I'd seen this report in the paper where Peter was supposed to have said to the board: "I either want first-team football, or I want to leave." When I saw that, I laughed. I thought, I've played for England and won a World Cup. Does he honestly think they're going to drop me and put him in? A couple of weeks later, Matt Gillies came to the training ground, which he never, ever did. We were running around the track, warming up. Before he even said a word, I knew exactly what was going to happen. He told me: 'The board have had a meeting. What would you think about leaving?' Straight away, I knew it was done, so I replied: 'Well, if that's all you think about me then I'll go.' It really shook me up – children, friends, social scene – we were really settled."

What were your options at that time?

"I'd heard rumours that Liverpool wanted me. Roger Hunt said don't sign for anyone because Bill Shankly is going to come in for you. Many years later, he did tell me that he went to his board but they refused him the money. Martin Peters told me that West Ham wanted me, but they signed Bobby Ferguson from Kilmarnock for £57,000 three weeks before I was put on the list. That was a lot of money. Stoke paid £50,000 for me."

Do you think you'd enjoy playing in the modern game?

"If you're talking about the work a goalkeeper has to do now, then no. If you're talking about the money, then yes! They've made it very difficult for goalkeepers now, with the light ball and people standing purposefully in front of the keeper at a corner. It's pure obstruction."

Do you have any regrets? Is there anything you wish you'd done differently?

"I wish I'd been a better driver! Although my career was cut short by my accident in 1972, I did go on to have a good few more years in the game, coaching at Stoke and playing in the NASL. No, to have a life in professional football was fabulous. Playing in front of thousands of people, enjoying every minute, and travelling all over the world into the bargain. Wearing the England shirt with that badge on it and standing there singing the National Anthem, I can't possibly have any regrets."

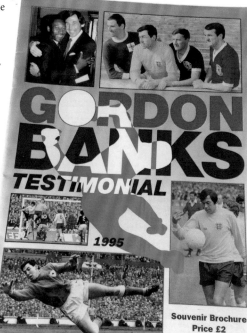

GORDON BANKS TESTIMONIAL

1995

Souvenir Brochure
Price £2

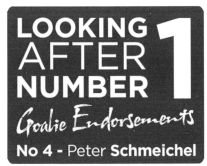

LOOKING AFTER NUMBER 1

Goalie Endorsements

No 4 - Peter Schmeichel

As one of the Premier League era's goalkeeping giants, Peter Schmeichel always came across as an admirably straight-shooting professional – hardly a man to be trifled with. Maybe it was the intense 'Great Dane' Scandinavian stereotype or his fiery on-field record as a stalwart of Manchester United's team of the 90s that gave us that warped

In 1997 he played second fiddle to the Honey Monster in fumbling a box of Sugar Puffs. Then he played butterfingers again, with a can of Pepsi, during a half-time roasting from Sir Alex.

Strangest of all, he played himself in a parallel universe – Peter Schmeichel, pig farmer – alone in a desolate Danish field, wondering what might have happened if he'd "bought some good-quality Reebok training kit instead of that cheap nylon rubbish."

The theme continued as a fancy-dress butcher

impression... because Schmeichel proved happy to vent a distinctly warped sense of humour in his forays into the world of advertising.

doing deadpan accordion song-and-dance numbers for Danepak bacon – which in turn stood him in good stead for some memorable appearances on *Strictly Come Dancing*...

GOALKEEPERS ARE DIFFERENT

It has long been acknowledged that goal-keepers are a funny lot. A breed apart, and usually more than a bit barking. Psychological extremes seem to come naturally with the territory. All alone in the six-yard box, the goalie is marked out by kit that is strikingly different to that of our team-mates – now usually fluorescent orange or violent puce – and voluntarily bears the crushing moral responsibility of

of thought supporting the argument that a goalkeeper isn't a footballer at all. We only ever master one kick, an insane boot into the stratosphere, with a ten-metre run-up. We gleefully shatter football's iron taboo every time we touch the ball with our hands – or even worse, with our giant banana-fingered gloves.

The most common perceived source of a goalkeeper's strangeness is the solitary nature of the specialist position. We can be seen as individuals in a team game. But we also have to be unusually brave to dive at forwards' feet, routinely putting our head in harm's way in the vicinity of lunging, studded boots. In some sense, we're anti-footballers, not directly contributing to the effort to score, but steadfastly doing our darnedest to prevent everyone else achieving the object of the game.

"Aloof, solitary, impassive, the crack goalie is followed in the streets by entranced small boys. He vies with the matador and the flying aces, an object of thrilled adulation. He is the lone eagle, the man of mystery, the last defender."

That's a heroic passage from *Speak, Memory*, the autobiography of Russian-American author Vladimir Nabokov, himself a not-so-Secret Goalie. It resurfaced recently in Jonathan Wilson's excellent *The Outsider*, which also focused on the psychology of keeping goal.

being the last line of defence.

Echoing the old rock 'n' roll argument that a drummer is merely a person who hangs out with musicians, there's a broad school

There's something about goalkeeping that tends to invite analysis of our state of mind, quite unlike any other position on the pitch. There's never been a book about playing left-back, never mind a film or a psychological study.

Like predatory cats, we keepers used to 'mark our territory' around the six-yard line and hang our lucky towel in the net; we still religiously kick the goalposts before taking a kick. According to Wolfson and Neave's landmark study of testosterone levels in sport (*Preparing For Home And Away Matches*, Northumbria University Human Cognitive Neuroscience Unit, 2004) we're frightened apes putting on a primitive display of territorial aggression: "Animals actually mark their territory with urine and other scents – this is unlikely to be acceptable in the away changing rooms, but some theorists contend that it might be useful for goalkeepers to leave their personal mark surreptitiously around their area on the pitch!"

You might think the shrinks were joking, but Argentinian keeper Sergio Goycoechea's penalty shootout tactics actually bore out their theory. In the 1990 World Cup semi against Yugoslavia, the call of nature forced him to take a sneaky wee on the pitch. "But we won, so then when the semi-final against Italy went to penalties I did it again – and it worked! So from that moment on I did it before every shoot-out. It was my lucky charm."

No one else on the football field employs superstitious rituals to the same extent as the goalkeeper. We put a voodoo hoodoo on penalty takers, and many of us still carry the magical tokens that used to belong in our mysterious glovebag.

The psychological pressures at play are varied and complex. We lead our defence from the rear with an optimal mix of shouting, pointing and clapping. We get the blame every time a goal is scored, but if we make a save it was savable, and so merely par for the course. If scoring a goal is often equated with sexual 'scoring', we are defenders of honour, obsessed with the virginal perfection of a 'clean sheet'.

The goalkeeper may be thought of as an ultra-defensive, negative presence or a crucial match-winner, with every shot saved counting the same as a goal scored. So goalkeeping is either a profoundly conservative, responsible, passive pastime – or the most pivotal, positive and confrontational position of all. That much, at least, is clear.

"I wore huge gloves to scare the opposition," Sepp Maier

TESTIMONIALS

There is no sadder day in any footballer's career than the testimonial match. Like any party without cause for celebration, the atmosphere is awkward, while the forced jollity of the occasion does nothing to mask the awful reality: it's all over.

The programme tributes and affectionate speeches over the Tannoy are heartfelt but uncomfortable, chiefly because the object of the shared memories and familiar anecdotes is actually present, like an uninvited guest at his own wake.

Just as any long-time employee collects his silver mantel clock for loyal service, the broken goalkeeper is also expected to run through his party tricks one last time.

The match will involve young, relevant team-mates, fellow faded club legends and TV celebrities (disc jockeys, members of the Rubettes) playing a pick-up XI representing his bitterest local rivals.

The final score will be 7-6, the game won in the last second of play by a penalty kick taken (retaken if necessary) by the object of the crowd's respectful charity. In Britain, we don't naturally 'do' public displays of sadness or affection – and likewise

fear of penury.

It's a good job, quite literally, that today's stars are all millionaire jet-setting playboys. No more testimonials. Cheerio, and good luck.

70

John Milkins
souvenir book

Mike Stowell Testimonial Match Sunday, July 30 Kick-off: 2pm

LIVER POOL
FOOTBALL CLUB

The
BRUCE GROBBELAAR
Testimonial Match
Official Souvenir Programme £1.00

1981-82
LEAGUE CHAMPIONS
& MILK CUP WINNERS

1982-83
LEAGUE CHAMPIONS
& MILK CUP WINNERS
CHARITY SHIELD WINNERS

1983-84
LEAGUE CHAMPIONS
& MILK CUP WINNERS
EUROPEAN CUP WINNERS

1984-85

1985-86
LEAGUE & CUP
DOUBLE

1986-87
CHARITY SHIELD
JOINT WINNERS

1987-88
LEAGUE CHAMPIONS

1988-89
F.A. CUP WINNERS
CHARITY SHIELD WINNERS

1989-90
LEAGUE CHAMPIONS
CHARITY SHIELD WINNERS

1990-91
LEAGUE RUNNERS-UP
CHARITY SHIELD JOINT WINNERS

1991-92
F.A. CUP WINNERS

1992-93
TESTIMONIAL MATCH

LIVERPOOL v EVERTON
Saturday 10th October 1992
Gates Open 12.15pm ... Kick Off 3pm

MATCH SPONSORS *Candy* AND **Manweb**

BRUCE GROBBELAAR *Eleven Great Years*

JOHN JACKSON
TESTIMONIAL MATCH

CRYSTAL PALACE v CHELSEA OFFICIAL PROGRAMME 10P

SKY BLUES v ENGLAND 1966 WORLD CUP XI

McFAUL

A Testimonial for WILLIE McFAUL
NEWCASTLE UNITED v MANCHESTER CITY   20p

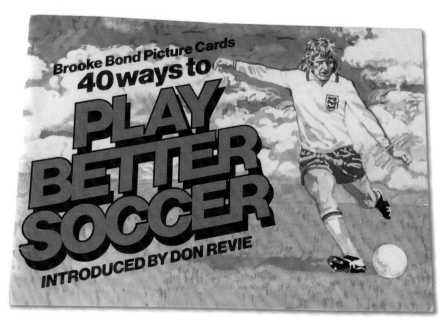

THE NAME'S BOND...
BROOKE BOND

Did you know that the Brooke Bond 'Play Better Soccer' set from 1976/77 is one of the most common in the whole history of football cards and stickers? The tea barons gave them away to millions of avid suppers for an extended period, making them extremely popular but wrecking their future price profile on eBay and at collector fairs.

Not only are the cards a lovely slice of 70s culture, they're also packed with invaluable tips for goalies that are still relevant today.

"Clemence has 'good' hands for catching", you'll learn on number 16: The High Catch. "It often looks as though he has glue on his palms to make the ball stick. He's the master of the high ball. Judging the flight of the ball with perfect concentration, ignoring any pressure from the opposing strikers he rises to grasp the ball. Forming a perfect cradle

with his hands, with his thumbs at the back of the ball, he pulls the ball down into his body as he drops to the ground. As he lands he will already be computing in his mind the opportunities for a swift counter attack."

You'll never fumble a centre again. You're probably already computing in your mind the plaudits this inside tip can win you during your next match. Whenever you're ready, let's move on to number 17: Goalkeeper's Punch.

"In the illustration a high corner has sailed across just outside the goal area. Clemence is hemmed in by both attacking

Ray's busy day: England appear to be overrun by an unidentified foreign power, possibly from behind the Iron Curtain.

40 WAYS TO
PLAY BETTER SOCCER

No. 31 GOALKEEPER CONTROL

Don Revie praises Ray Clemence, England goalkeeper, as "the governor of the penalty box". Clemence dominates the area round his goal. His team mates leave well alone when he shouts a ball is "his"!

When a free kick is taken against England just outside the England penalty area it's Clemence who organises the precise positioning of the defensive wall, using one of the England strikers who has dropped back to help him by marking the position of the dead ball.

In this picture Clemence has darted off his goal line to gather a ball bouncing around dangerously in his penalty area after the break-down of an opponents' set-piece attack from a free kick.

Picture Cards 16 and 17 demonstrate Ray Clemence dealing with high balls in his area with equal determination.

Save these cards in a Play Better Soccer Album introduced by England Team Manager Don Revie.

It's Free from grocers when you buy ¼lb of PG Tips tea or send 6½p postage to Brooke Bond Oxo Ltd, Parkway House Sheen Lane, London SW14 8LU

Cards included Free with Brooke Bond PG Tips Tea and Tea Bags.

gain those vital inches to clear his goal.

"On other occasions the high ball will be threatening the goal direct, and at these times, as Don Revie, England's manager says, 'Clemence is exceptional at going back five paces and flicking over the bar the floater or the drifter.'" *

These collector cards may be priceless for sentimental reasons and for top-notch tip absorption, but they're pretty much valueless cashwise. You should be able to pick up the complete set in the album for around a quid. Go get 'em, shot-stoppers.

* Other soul groups of the 60s and 70s are available.

players and defenders. Once he has decided to go for the ball and has left his goal line Clemence is totally deter- mined to reach the ball before anyone else. Here you see him having to use just one fist to achieve maximum reach and

SONDICO SPORTS

Most people today would probably associate Sondico with Sports Direct, but it wasn't always this way. Sondico Sports was kicked off back in 1946 by the Sondhi family, who produced everything from shuttlecocks to cricket bats. In the 70s they started to manufacture cheap string gloves in their Indian factory, rivalling the smooth cotton Peter Bonetti brand.

In 1971 their first advert in *Charles Buchan's Football Monthly* had no sign of gloves, just a 32-panel football to whet the whistle. Only seven years later did they start selling gloves with a player's endorsement, Peter Shilton being just the first great goalie to star in Sondico magazine ads.

RAY CLEMENCE

KELHAM O'HANLON

JOE CORRIGAN

PETER HUCKER

NIGEL SPINK

Sondico

BOB BOLDER

IAN HESFORD

CHRIS WOODS

The Professional Choice

Clemence and Corrigan soon completed the brand's clean sweep of England's three keepers.

At this time an order-sheet code would identify the international origin and quality of the gloves. India (GI) and Hong Kong (GH) were trumped by Germany (GG), the highest quality gloves sported by the professionals, well out of the price range of wannabe kids and parents grateful for the lower-end options.

In the 80s more keepers started wearing the double SS brand. Nigel Spink gave the gloves some great exposure coming on as sub for the injured Jimmy Rimmer in the 1982 European Cup Final, while QPR's Peter Hucker produced Man of the Match performances in the same year's FA Cup final.

"On the eve of the final," Hucker reveals, "Sondico sent me a couple of pairs of new silver-and black-gloves which they wanted me to wear. After a little 'discussion', I pointed out that I'd never wear an untried glove – which wouldn't look good should I let one or two goals slip

through my fingers! So we decided I would
wear the black-and-silver for the warm up
but revert to the trusted red ones for the
game. For the replay I actually decided to
wear the new gloves, but not before having a
few training sessions to get used to them!"

In the 90s came the Sondico Goalkeeping
School. A quarterly magazine, *Between the
Posts*, was produced complete with member-
ship card, discounts and exclusive offers.

More Wembley appearances and
European cup finals followed and the stable
of keepers grew even stronger. Neville
Southall, Chris Woods, David James, Tony
Coton and Andy Goram all had gloves made
in their name – though interestingly, their
names never actually appeared on the gloves
– with the introduction of some true classic
designs and styles.

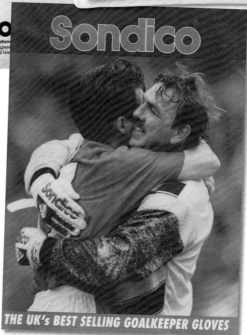

75

LOOKING AFTER NUMBER 1

Goalie Endorsements

No 5 - Peter Mellor

Back in the 70s and 80s, Peter Mellor stood out as a huge character with an infectious enthusiasm for football, goalkeeping and fun. We knew there was something a bit different about him when, before a game, the Fratton End crowd used to chant "Peter, Peter throw us some sweets" – and he did. A spirited entrepreneur, he

telephone number in the ad alongside his sparkling white Rolls-Royce Silver Shadow. He was ahead of his time as an entrepreneur, holding goalkeeping schools in Portsmouth for budding keepers. And after finishing his long career in America playing for the Edmonton Drillers, he then started up a beach soccer company which is still going strong today.

Mellor's many lovable eccentricities included a radio show called 'Mellow Mellor' on the Portsmouth's local Radio Victory, where he would interview showbiz personalities. We asked Peter about it when we spoke to him recently.

"It meant I could play for the Commentators and Showbiz XI," he fondly recalled. "It was at that time that I managed to buy a house in America, and I fell in love with the place. I had lots of other jobs before the beach soccer was set up, which even included maintaining swimming pools."

As well as running goalie schools in Portsmouth, business-minded Peter used

always seemed to be up to some wizard wheeze or another.

Peter advertised his chauffeur service in the Portsmouth club programme, rather touchingly using his own home

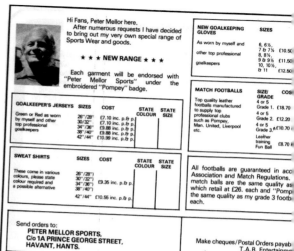

to run a sports shop selling gloves and jerseys with the (now ultra-rare!) Peter Mellor logo.

"When I was at Portsmouth," he told us, "Gola brought out a range of goalkeeping gloves in addition to their kit and boots. They were already manufacturing a woollen glove, the 'Taki', but wanted to compete with the likes of Uhlsport and Reusch. They asked me to use them and give feedback – they weren't particularly well made but were a step up, for sure. I'd previously experimented with Adidas

gloves just prior to this which Alan Knight was also wearing. Before this we would have appeals in the club programme to help us with purchasing gloves as the club was reluctant to fund us – and the decent ones weren't cheap!"

"When I was at Fulham, both Peter Shilton and Peter Bonetti gave me cotton gloves they both endorsed – so one week I would wear Peter Shilton's yellow ones and the following week Peter's green pair. Even the commentator on *Match of the Day* picked up on this and said, "I wonder what colour gloves Peter Mellor is going to be wearing this week!"

We could fill pages with Peter's stories - getting the PFA to fund his flying lessons was another of his cracking ideas – but let's finish off with his top tip for budding goalies.

"I took up knitting as a child," says the great showman unexpectedly. "It helps to keep your fingers strong and supple."

John Burridge

"Mine were a pair of Adidas Curkovic, which I got whilst playing in Bilbao in a pre-season friendly. I was one of the first keepers in Britain to wear these latex-palmed gloves in the 70s and I even ended up selling to fellow keepers as they were so hard to get hold of. One of the best gloves I wore too - loved them!"

JOHN BURRIDGE
ASTON VILLA
GOALKEEPER

What can you say about John Burridge that hasn't been heard before? He wasn't just a great keeper but a one-man inspiration for countless astonishing anecdotes.

Everyone knows about the goalkeeping career spanning four decades and 29 clubs. The pre-match warm-up tumbling displays. Budgie watching *Match of the Day* in his gloves, holding on to a size 5 Mitre football. Having his wife throwing him oranges at the dinner table to keep his reflexes sharp. Sleeping naked apart from his Uhlsport gloves and giving imaginary interviews to Gerald Sinstadt while talking in his sleep.

But what about the Shilton tribute hairdo? Surely that couldn't be true, we asked, personally giving John the chance to set the record straight.

"Oh yes, I took a photo of Peter Shilton in to a local hairdressers so I could have the same perm. Shilts was my hero. I got it done before the last game of the season for Palace against Burnley, the year we won promotion. That game is up there as one of my most memorable games. I conceded 24 goals and kept 24 clean sheets. We had a great team and under Terry Venables we had a top-class manager. The best I've ever played for!"

And what about the little-known spell that Budgie had playing at Portsmouth, just prior to signing for Southampton back in 1987?

It was a hot summer afternoon on Southsea Common, and Paul Thomas and his Pompey-mad mates were enjoying a kick-around before retiring to a seafront juicer. No one was too put out when a bypasser asked if he could join in. Although it did seem a bit strange how he left his wife sitting on a bench, casually reading a newspaper. And he did seem somehow familiar...

"Like a true pro, John got straight down to business," Paul told us. "He took off his jumper and set about playing centre-forward. And before we knew it he was screaming for the ball and making us chase down opponents." "He was superb, John. The lads still talk about it to this day. What we didn't know at the time was that he was signing for Saints the next day. If we had, we might have left

more of an impression on him, in more ways than one!"

We asked Budgie if he remembered the incident. "I just loved playing football," he said. "And this wasn't the only time I stopped for a kickabout with lads like this."

Cue another fantastic story we heard from Andy Hall of Tamworth. Andy was 10 in 1976 when he got a new pair of Clarks football boots, complete with a card with

NEWCASTLE UNITED

us, with a cheeky grin and smile for us to see. After time I summon up the courage to ask Budgie if he'll sign my Clarks football card – and he gives me a goalkeeper's glove, too. I felt like I was the luckiest lad on earth. He even came over to Tamworth in his TR7 to play in park matches

a space for your favourite player's autograph. No problem, reckon Andy's mates Tim, Mark and Max, who happen to have heard that Villa's new signing Budgie has moved into a house in Eldon.

One five-mile pilgrimage later, the four hot and sweaty boys have not only magically located the house, but Budgie has also asked them in for drink, and to meet his wife! And so the cycle trip becomes a weekly fixture, to play football with Budgie in his back garden.

"Budgie kicks the ball over a neighbour's fence and apologises," Andy recalls, "blaming

with us – never in goal, always playing out!

"John Burridge, you are an idol, you'll never know how much your kindness and gener-osity was welcomed and idolised by us lads. Forty-two years on I have never forgotten these summer bike rides."

PARK LIFE

Oh, to be a Premier League goalie, prowling around your box like a ninja supermodel while your world-class mates keep the ball down the other end for whole halves at a time. The lucky sods. A Premier League goalie wouldn't last two seconds in grassroots football, down in the weedy foundations of the football pyramid. They wouldn't like it when there's kids kicking into the back of your net, or having to put the nets up, or having not a single blade of grass in your area.

They couldn't handle the pensioners who come over for a chat, or having to take the nets down and getting all stuck up with used sock tape, or the dog-walkers cutting across the corner of the pitch when someone's trying to take a corner.

And then there's the dogs running off their leads, wanting to play ball. Your Premier League superstar wouldn't stand a chance. The wide open spaces of the council pitches, and your two posts just crying out like they're a natural target.

The Greatest SAVES

No 5

PAT JENNINGS
LIVERPOOL 1-1 TOTTENHAM
Date: 31 March 1973
Venue: Anfield

"Did you ever see the likes of that?" asked Bill Shankly. "Did you ever see anything so incredible?"

The focus of the great Liverpool boss's admiration and frustration was Tottenham goalkeeper Pat Jennings, who had just sensationally deprived the Reds of a vital home point in their title bid.

Jennings had been all but unbeatable all morning, thoroughly eclipsing the spectacle of the Grand National later that day. Somehow, he stopped a seemingly endless salvo of shots and headers, along with two penalty kicks. Kevin Keegan saw Jennings dive to his right to palm away the first; so Tommy Smith hit the next one to Pat's left, with identical results.

As Jennings leapt to his feet, punching the air with delight, 'The Anfield Iron' sank to his knees and pounded the ground with his fists. Referee Bob Raby just stood and shook his head, grinning in wonder at what he was witnessing.

Even the Ref applauded!...

CORINTHIAN CUSTODIANS

Any keen collector will know that the first Corinthian keeper was a yellow-shirted David Seaman in the 'Headliner' set of 16 bulbous-bonced England stars in 1995.

But were you aware that the 1996 FAPL Collection missed out models for Tony Coton (Manchester City), Dave Beasant (Southampton) and Alan Miller (Middlesbrough), despite including them in the promotional book?

We asked Alan Miller about the oversight: no goalie for Boro!

"This is something that keeps me awake most nights!" he revealed exclusively.

A *Who's Who?* of British goalkeeping. Literally.

GOALKEEPING SCHOOL

The Bob Wilson Goalkeeping School ran from 1983 to 1997, during which time it provided an oasis of top-class, personal tutelage that must have seemed like a dream come true for many aspiring schoolboy keepers. Just imagine being whisked away in the middle of the school holidays to the goalkeeping equivalent of Hogwart's...

Bob told us that he was originally driven to set up the courses because: "Specialised goalkeeping coaching tended to be overlooked compared to outfield play. Yet goalkeeping is the most specialised position on the pitch."

The summer camps started up in the grounds of Middlesex Polytechnic, costing £120 for a week's course, or £77 without the sleepovers.

"I made sure that I was always available on course days," Bob said. "If you run a course in your own name, it was only right that you should

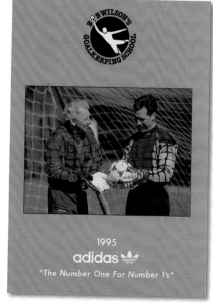

1995

adidas

"The Number One For Number 1's"

be on hand and be very much involved when the course takes place."

Bob was assisted by an amazing group of coaches and staff to look after the

Comedian Lenny Sherman lent us his sweatshirt. "I had a brilliant week and loved every minute. I still talk about it today!"

kids during their stay. Celebrity guests such as David Seaman, Hans Segers, Joe Corrigan, Pat Jennings and John Lukic would then turn up for Q&A sessions – plus visits to watch games at Arsenal or Spurs came as part of the course.

Given the privilege of leafing through Bob's course notes and pamphlets today – 'Making decisions: catch, block or deflect'; 'Keep the head steady and the neck screwed in tight'; 'Presentation of certificates on the final afternoon' – it's no wonder that he's still stopped in the street by nostalgic former students.

If only there were an adult version, we'd all sign up in a jiffy.

BOB WILSON'S GOALKEEPING SCHOOL

difficulty of getting grass and mud stains out, and here was a marketing opportunity that would literally make his client stand out from the crowd.

It wasn't long before Jon and Peter were breezing into reception at the Admiral HQ in Wigston for a meeting with company chief Bert Patrick.

The result was a white roll-necked shirt with a combined Admiral/PS logo which was an instant hit with the kids.

This, in the days when keepers wore the same shorts and socks as the rest of team, meant that Shilton cut quite a majestic figure in his all-white Leicester strip.

Formerly Cook & Hurst, manufacturers of underwear for sixty years, Admiral moved into football kit production after taking on overflow work from Umbro and Bukta.

The Man in White: Shilton acquires a saintly glow.

ADMIRAL

Back in the early 1970s, Jon Holmes, Peter Shilton's agent, was flicking through *The Observer's Book of Association Football* when he paused on the page that showed the limited colour range of jerseys that goalkeepers were allowed to wear.

Yellow was for 'Internationals only', green, blue, red and... white.

It struck Holmes that no keeper ever wore white, perhaps due to the

Fuelled by Patrick's energetic and innovative marketing ideas, Admiral began to revolutionise the relationship between clubs and their kit suppliers, bringing in a whole new level of commercialism.

The Admiral logo was soon being worn by Leeds, Manchester United, England, Wales, West Ham, Norwich, Tottenham, Leicester and many other teams. The kit designs were seen as quite outlandish at the time (though are now rightly viewed as design classics), but this didn't extend to the keeper jerseys, which remained quite conservative, with a standard button up collar design. Only the hugely popular England shirt had an element of design, with the twin black stripes down the sleeve and black cuffs, to match black shorts and socks, with Wales wearing the same, but with logos on the collar.

Sadly, by 1980 the company went into financial difficulties and were bought out by Dutch company Frisol Oil. Although the brand continued, the Golden Age of Admiral was over.

As for Shilton's all-white strip: it was abandoned after Kevin Keegan lobbed

GOALKEEPERS JERSEYS

Big name goalkeepers like Ray Clemence, England; Peter Shilton, England and Stoke; David Harvey, Leeds and Scotland and Alec Stepney, Manchester United, all wear Admiral goalkeeping outfits. The England goalkeepers jersey is made from 100% polyester Airflow fabric and comes complete with the England badge. Small boys', Boys', Youths', Small Men's, Men's, Large.

ENGLAND GOALKEEPER ALL SIZES 518

ROYAL 503 RED 501 EMERALD 500 · 519 WALES ALL SIZES · LEAGUE ALL SIZES · ROYAL 515 EMERALD 512 · ROYAL 508 RED 507 AMBER 509 EMERALD 505

Peter Shilton designs his own jersey with comfortable turtle neck also made from 100% polyester Airflow fabric. Non-restricting sleeves with Shilton badge on the chest. Small boys', Boys', Youths', Small Men's, Men's, Large.

Also available the new Welsh goalkeepers jerseys in the same style as England but in Sky Blue with Black trimmings down the sleeves with Welsh badge, of course.

Our league quality goalkeepers jersey is worn by many top-notch keepers including David Harvey and Alec Stepney. In plain colours with button front neck and collar. Made from 100% polyester Airflow fabric with non-restrictive sleeves.

The Admiral conventional 'Y' insert style goalkeepers jersey is made in 100% polyester Airflow fabric with Admiral badge on chest. Sizes: Small boys', Boys', Youths', Small Men's, Men's, and Large.

him in an FA Cup semi-final replay under lights at Villa Park, and it was claimed that the kit had made the Leicester keeper easier to see!

COVER STARS

"One can never get that excited about seeing goalkeepers live," Nick Hornby opined. "They're like newsreaders, or weather forecasters: the chances are, you've seen them 7,000 times before. If you nodded off for a few minutes then you missed George Best's entire career, but even Rip van Winkle would have caught up with Peter Shilton

"You only end up in goal," Hornby concluded, "if you are a) small, b) bad at football, c) easily intimidated by your peers, or d) carrying a minor leg injury. So it is

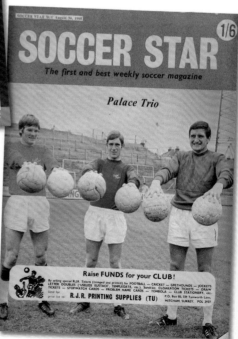

somewhere along the line.

Hornby wrote his article, 'Who Wants to Go in Goal? Not Me', in 1996. When this particular issue of *Esquire* appeared, it was like 99.9% of football, sports and men's magazines. It did not feature a goalkeeper on the cover. You'll already know the reason why from previous experience of vintage banter: goalkeepers are just like the drummers in bands. They're not real musicians/football stars.

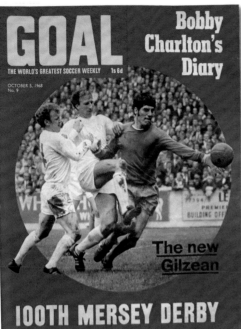

GOAL
THE WORLD'S GREATEST SOCCER WEEKLY 1s 6d

OCTOBER 5, 1968
No. 9

Bobby
Charlton's
Diary

The new
Gilzean

100TH MERSEY DERBY

somewhat surprising that goalkepers end
up as six-foot-nine megalomaniacs with no
discernible limp whatsoever."

WORLD CUP COLD WAR AGAINST GOLAC

SHOOT! 25p
11th APRIL, 1981

Vote for
SHOOT'S
Most Exciting
Players
of the Year

**Paul
Cooper**
—England's
safest 'keeper

'NO CRISIS
AT ARSENAL'
—John Hollins

EURO CUPS
Semi-Finals

JORDAN
DEFENDS
BIRTLES

10 West Germany
adidas shirts
to be won

Australia—50c; New Zealand—50c; Malaysia—$1.70; Italy—L.1,200; Denmark—Kr.11.00

FREE SOCCER DIPLOMA OFFER

FOOTBALL
WORLD'S GREATEST SOCCER MONTHLY
VOLUME 7 NUMBER 2 SEPTEMBER 1980 50p

LEICESTER
COLOUR ALBUM

MAN. UTD.
SEXTON'S PLEDGE

SPURS
ARCHIBALD'S PROGRESS

VILLA
UNLUCKY LITTLE

BRIGHTON
HARD GOAL FACTS

BIRMINGHAM
ARCHIE'S BACK!

PLUS FREE PRIZE CONTESTS
...ENGLAND MANAGERS' SURVEY

onze

POSTER HISTORIQUE: LES 20 GARDIENS DE DIVISION 1
STRASBOURG CLUB DU MOIS
LES VERTS A SALONIQUE • WOODCOCK A COLOGNE • MAIER RETROUVÉ

Mark Wallington spreads the
message of peace and love.

CEREAL OFFENDERS

Before setting off to school, there's nothing better to set up your day than finding a small plastic giveaway toy in your cornflakes. Back in the 70s, Shredded Wheat made the experience all the more thrilling by including actual life-size World Cup final seats in the box and handing out football stickers to fill up your Bob Wilson Soccer Action album.

When you realise that you haven't seen the word 'Welgar' in decades.

The only slight downside was having to eat the Shredded Wheat themselves, a funny old-fash-ioned hybrid of a haystack and a mattress.

All you have to do to enter the Banksy competition is to shuffle these Goalkeeping Skills into the correct order – Concentration, Confidence, Determination, Fast Reflexes, Fitness and Positional Sense. Then complete this sentence in 12 words: "Gordon Banks is one of the world's most gifted and respected footballers because..."

Send your answers to Nabisco, complete with TWO Shredded Wheat packet tops. Contest closes April 30th 1974 and is open to UK residents only. Come on, England!

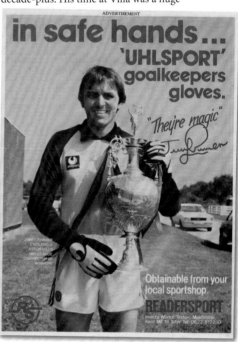

in safe hands...
'UHLSPORT'
goalkeepers gloves.

"They're magic"

JIMMY RIMMER
ENGLAND &
ASTON VILLA
1981 LEAGUE
CHAMPIONSHIP
WINNER

Obtainable from your local sportshop.

READERSPORT
Invicta Works, Teston, Maidstone, Kent ME18 5NW Tel: 0622 812250

Among the earliest and most enthusiastic adopters of goalkeeper gloves was Aston Villa's Jimmy Rimmer. The former Manchester United and Arsenal keeper started his career when the best gloves on offer were made of cotton with pimpled rubber strips, so it's no surprise that he embraced the new latex-palm technology. At a personal high point he used to carry no fewer than TEN pairs of his beloved Uhlsport gloves on to the pitch with him – stuffed into his new and highly fashionable glovebag accessory.

The *Daily Mail* even took the unusual step of doing a feature on Jimmy and his exotic gloves, given the attention they were bringing. 'The Man with the Golden Gloves' article represented a major pay-off for Uhlsport, having chosen Rimmer as the first British keeper to exclusively promote their gloves and jerseys. 'A handy new trend helps Rimmer strengthen Villa's grip on the top...'

After coming up through the youth ranks at Old Trafford, Rimmer found his first-team chances limited due to the consistency of Alex Stepney. A loan spell at Swansea convinced Arsenal he was the man to replace the ageing Bob Wilson, and after he retired at the end of the 1973-74 season, Rimmer took over and held the number one jersey for the next three seasons, during which time he made his one and only appearance for England.

He looked set for a bright, long-term stay at Highbury, but when Terry Neill came in from Tottenham as manager, he brought with him one Pat Jennings. So Rimmer moved on again, this time to Aston Villa, where he became a fixture for the next half decade-plus. His time at Villa was a huge success, and included winning the old First Division title in season 1980-81.

But Rimmer suffered the cruellest of fates when, on the night of Villa's greatest triumph, he was injured only nine minutes into the 1982 European Cup Final, and had to be replaced. His understudy, Nigel Spink, turned in a heroic performance, hastening his own ascendancy to the Villa number one jersey. After another spell at Swansea, Jimmy Rimmer retired in 1986.

91

"Hey Colin, the kitman's only given me the mascot's shorts again!"

THE BLAME GAME

We're really sorry to have to break this awkward news, which may come as a terrible shock to many a proud keeper. It's on the subject of football, and how teams aren't just set up to prevent goals being scored. It turns out there's a whole secondary aspect to the game which involves actually trying to get the ball in the net. You know, that cue for fist-pumping and joyful celebration when it happens at the other end of the field?

Now, here's the thing. Occasionally, there will be a shot on goal at your end.

That's right. Through no fault of your defenders, your closing-down midfielders or tracking-back attackers, one of the oppo might elect to have a pop. He/she might even score. Please be calm, now. Take a deep breath and try to relax.

We are, of course, only joking.

Every proper, steadfast, dyed-in-the-nylon goalkeeper knows in their heart that no shot on goal is ever admissable in any circumstances. A shot on goal is an abomination. A disgrace. A scandal.

And someone out there on the pitch wearing [insert your team colours here] is to blame, right?

The next time some distracted, lazy, clueless team-mate allows a shot to threaten your goal, the only reasonable response is to take a masterclass from the great Peter Schmeichel, following the lead of Sir Alex Ferguson in his 'teacups' era. Pursue and bellow at the idiot responsible as if he were Steve Bruce.

Or else you could take things one step further, and handle the situation in the manner associated with Bruce Grobbelaar, a goalie who shall forever remain blameless.

His textbook study in blame and blamelessness came in a Merseyside derby away match back in 1993, when the waiflike Steve McManaman had the misfortune to make a rather poor clearance.

Wave your arms like a mad windmill and poke your culprit in the cheek.

Shout in your victim's face, and push their head backwards with your big glove. Make a grab for the throat.

Keep pointing and threatening and blaming even as the miserable wretch slopes back up the field for the restart.

There, that feels better now, doesn't it?

Tranmere Rovers' Eric Nixon administers a stern ticking-off.

93

IF THE CAP FITS

Once upon a time in Great British history, many a fellow could effortlessly be positioned in terms of occupation, class and income by the headwear he sported on an everyday basis. The City gent in his bowler. The miner in his safety helmet. The chef and the big train driver. The football hooligan and the judge.

Before the Second World War, the goalkeeper used to be instantly recognisable because he always wore a classic flat cap. The proof of the pudding came in the form of the eponymous Andy Capp, the *Daily Mirror's* throwback cartoon character who, you may remember, himself played in goal at the weekend, a cigarette dangling eternally from his lower lip. From the 50s right through to the 70s, the standard cartoon depiction of a keeper was a bloke leaning on his post wearing a flat or peaked cap. And then suddenly it wasn't.

Just as policemen no longer wear those pointy old helmets, it's incredibly rare to see a modern-day goalie wearing the peaked cap that bears his very name, as nature intended. It's hard to say why the fashion changed, because the cap was never a fashion item in the first place. It was always considered a practical necessity when the early-season sun sank low in the sky over the West Stand; and in the winter it kept your noggin warm.

Maybe it's something to do with hair gel, and the universal dread of being seen on a sports field with flat, tired or lifeless hair? Maybe you were born with it, maybe it's Maybelline.

In any case, one minute it was possible to buy Subbuteo goalies specially made with miniature peaked caps, and then – just glance away for 40 years and the toy manufacturers will always try to catch

J DAWSON. BURNLEY.

OGDEN'S CIGARETTES.

Bob Wilson
and Gordon
West:
from The
Wonderful
World of
Caps, FKS
1972/73.

you out – they
were sneak-
ily withdrawn
from stock,
never to be
produced
again.

Nowadays,
goalkeep-
ers prefer to
hold a hand
up to keep
the sun out
of their eyes
– which is fine until they're motivated
to move their handy temporary sunshade
by the prospect of a football hurtling toward
the angle of their upright at 75mph. They
move their hand, they can't see. One-nil. But
at least they've got a ready-made excuse.

Into the vacuum left by the goalie's cap, a
number of individual alternatives have appeared over the years. While John Burridge's
occasional donning of a sun visor undoubtedly scored high in the sartorial stakes, the
coolest of these must surely be the protective
headgear adopted by American national
goalie Alan Mayer in the NASL. Long before
Petr Cech was advised by his doctors to take
precautions to avoid another dangerous
blow to the head, Mayer of the San Diego
Sockers cheated forwards' flying feet by donning a regular padded skateboard helmet.

It's never too late to start a new trend, or
to revive an old one.

OTHER HEADGEAR
IS AVAILABLE

JOHN **BURRIDGE -**
Old lady golfer's sun visor

PETR **CECH -**
Vintage rugby headguard

JENS MARTIN **KNUDSEN**
Cheeky bobble hat

The Greatest SAVES

No 6

RENE HIGUITA
ENGLAND 0-0 COLOMBIA
Date: 6 September 1995
Venue: Wembley Stadium

Here's a rarity in any cavalcade of famous and fantastic saves: a stop in an otherwise forgettable friendly international, made when the ball wasn't even in play, but which nevertheless went on to change the goalkeeping landscape. Especially that part which involves small boys messing around in the playground.

Looking for all the world like the Friendly Lion in The Wizard of Oz, the Colombian keeper carried into the match an eccentric reputation even on the South American scale, but left it a lasting global legend.

A harmless cross by England debutant Frank Lampard floated toward Higuita's goal, who alone had noticed the linesman flagging for an incidental offside. But instead of simply catching the ball and returning it to a team-mate, Higuita startled everyone watching by flicking his legs up behind him and volleying the ball away with the soles of his boots. It wasn't the first Scorpion Kick the game had seen – he'd practised it a few times earlier during the warm-up – and it certainly would not be the last.

The Scorpion...

RENÉ HIGUITA

A BIT OF AN ANIMAL

Stand-up comedian Stewart Lee isn't much of a football fan, but he's got a great story about his old flatmate and his nickname for Peter Shilton: 'The Bee'. It's based on the established scientific fact that a bumblebee's tiny wings should not, according to the laws of physics, be able to lift their owner off the

PLAYER'S CIGARETTES

LONG-HAIRED BLACK

ground. And neither should a hulking 6'1", 14-stone bodybuilder be able to fly through the air to tip an incoming cannonball around his upright. It's just not possible. And so, 'The Bee'.

This is just one of a hundred great goalie nicknames which spookily all have one thing in common. Every single keeper you can think of is nicknamed after a favourite from the animal kingdom.

Okay, let's get the easiest one out of the way first. No, not Billy 'The Fish' Thompson, we meant Peter 'The Cat' Bonetti. So called because of the large flap in his back door (though never, ever in his area).

Starting at the level of all-time world greats and working slowly down through the animal-related legends, there's Lev 'The Black Octopus' Yashin, José-Luis 'The Bulldog' Chilavert and the irrepressible John 'Budgie' Burridge.

Then there was Edwin 'Dumbo' van der Sar and Piet 'The Bear' Schrijvers (both Ajax & Holland), Marcus 'Red Bird' Hahnemann (Reading & USA), Tommy 'The Flying Pig' Lawrence (Liverpool), Walter 'Spiderman' Zenga (Inter) and his hapless 7-foot relative Zeljko 'Spider' Kalac (Leicester City & Australia).

Finally, here's all the best ones we surreptitiously looked up on the excellent Goalkeepers Are Different blog: Theo 'The Walrus' Custers (Espanyol & Belgium), Dragoje 'The Eel' Leković (Kilmarnock & Yugoslavia), Ubaldo 'The Duck' Fillol (River Plate & Argentina), Oscar 'The Rabbit' Peréz (Cruz Arul & Mexico) and his thematic understudy, Carlos 'Lettuce' Roa (Argentina).

Ah yes, and not forgetting David 'H' Seaman. The exception that proves the rule.

I Am the Walrus: go compare on p124.

PLAYER'S CIGARETTES.

WILD DUCK.
OR MALLARD.

BULL DOG.

LOOKING AFTER NUMBER 1

Goalie Endorsements

No 6 - Peter Shilton

Without wishing to boast or pull rank on less fortunate mortals, some of us were ac-

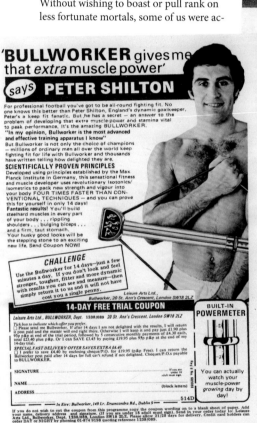

endorsement circles, this was the equivalent of seeing Sex Pistols at Manchester's Free Trade Hall five years later. It was like standing alongside Neil Armstrong when he fluffed his lines on the moon.

Some of us queued up nervously with our mum to meet the great man. He was much bigger up close than viewed from the middle of the Double Decker. And some of us not only got to shake his hand but were also gifted a free Schick razor postcard (got) and a personally signed poster of Pete wearing a black Admiral shirt with a red-and-green sash (on wall throughout childhood, not got).

Since that day, the thrill of meeting Peter Shilton and playing a small but key role in football's nascent merchandising industry has only been matched once. In retrospect, it's probably just as well it wasn't at the advent of Shilton's stint as the face (and upper torso) of Bullworker, despite the scientifically proven protestations of the Max Planck Institute.

A couple of years later, at the Card Shop in Oadby, some of us actually got to meet Orinoco Womble. In the flesh (okay, in the man-sized Womble suit). And some of us even had the wherewithal to go round twice.

tually there at the Woolco department store in Oadby, Leicester, in sunny 1972. In goalie

TRACKY BOTTOMS

Late last century, tracky bottoms were part of every goalie's sartorial armoury, come the winter months. But in more recent years they've become the goalkeeping equivalent of plus-fours.

The main reason they used to see so much duty was of course as protection against hard, frozen pitches. Blame it on global warming that thousands of pairs of surplus tracky bottoms are now stored in the back of garages along with lonely sledges.

Every bit as popular in their time as global

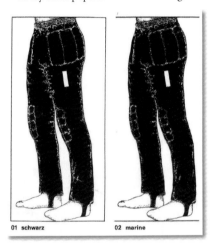

01 schwarz   02 marine

tracky bottom stylist of all. "It started 20 years ago, these grey bottoms," Hungary keeper Gabor Kiraly told the Beeb during Euro 2016. "It began in Hungary and it brought me luck" – and likewise at Hertha Berlin and Crystal Palace.

"You can't just put grey bottoms on in goal (to play well), you have to move your bottom. I want to work and I can only do this in these grey bottoms. I play 20 years in these bottoms for Hungary and I don't think I'll be changing."

warming today, the plastic pitches of the 80s also made tracky bottoms a necessity. Astroturf was concrete with a quarter-inch layer of luminous green carpet laid on top. It made a goalie's life hell with carpet burns, bruised knees, hips and elbows. "The plastic pitch was one of the reasons I moved on from QPR," serial tracky offender John Burridge revealed exclusively to us. "I hated that pitch so much!"

Chelsea keeper Dimitri Kharine provides us with another reason for 'bottoming up' no matter what the weather. He'd suffered bad knee injuries at CSKA Moscow prior to his 1992 move to Chelsea, and wore them to protect the scar tissue.

And so to the most famous modern-day

FIRST GLOVE

Neville Southall
"My first pair were the green cotton gloves, I then started using a pair which were black and white, the Uhlsport 025, which I bought myself. After that Phil Parkes got me a sponsorship deal with Sukan Sports when I was at Everton. He was a great guy, helping me when he didn't have to."

BEASANT

Everybody knows that Dave Beasant was the first man to save a penalty in an FA Cup Final, diving to deny John Aldridge when he appeared for plucky Wimbledon against

Over to Dave and his 30-year-old party-piece to see if we can coax you into agreement.

"I got to wear Cannonball gloves when the owner of the company asked to come to Wimbledon to show me 'The Cannonball'," Dave remembers.

The Cannonball Kid.

mighty Liverpool back in 1988. And everybody knows that 'Lurch' was the first goalkeeping captain to lift the FA Cup... but did you know he was the first to get paid in gloves for doing both?

We met up with Dave to whisk him back in time to that Wembley afternoon, and enjoy the chance to ask him first-hand about the Cannonball glove story – one of the greatest forgotten stories in goalkeeping paraphernalia history. In our opinion.

"This was a machine that would serve balls for a goalkeeper, much the same as the machine that does it for tennis and now cricket."

"Problem was, this machine had to be

100

towed on the back of a car! These were the days before goalkeeping coaches were in at many clubs, but the cost of this machine was so expensive you could have hired a full-time coach instead."

"Gordon Banks came to do a session with me using the machine, and when we got our heads together, we thought a good way of getting the brand known would be to make a glove – call them Cannonball, and I would wear them. The thing was, the company wanted an incentive-based contract, and at that time, the FA Cup was huge in Scandinavia."

So you signed a contract that offered more money the further Wimbledon went in the Cup? They were probably hoping you'd reach the fifth round.

"A lot was based on results in that one competition, with further bonuses for clean sheets and penalty saves, going up each time the further we progressed – and, of course, we all know we reached the final, and what happened there!"

You must have thought you'd hit the jackpot, financially?

"I did hit the jackpot. But unfortunately Cannonball couldn't afford to pay me..."

That's right. Wimbledon winning the Cup with Dave's bonus penalty save actually caused a problem for his glove company. But there's a happy ending of sorts to this adventure in sports marketing.

"So they just gave me all the gloves they'd made!"

It was a fitting end to a classic underdog story at Wembley. The Crazy Gang versus the superstars. The record-breaking penalty save. The joy and adulation of lifting the FA Cup in Cannonball gloves.

And a warehouse full of them to remember the day by.

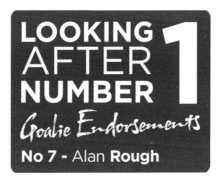

LOOKING AFTER NUMBER 1

Goalie Endorsements

No 7 - Alan **Rough**

On the grand scale of football endorsements, it may not be up there with the all-time glamour money-spinners, but there was an irresistible synergy between the Scotland keeper and a car showroom in Hamilton.

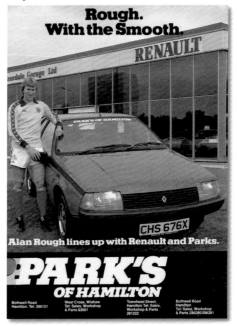

Rough. With the Smooth.

Alan Rough lines up with Renault and Parks.

PARK'S OF HAMILTON

Rough. With the Smooth. Geddit?

It may not look much now, but back in 1981 the X-reg Renault 18 was about as plush a motor as was available north of the border. Especially to a man wearing full kit in the street of a Tuesday afternoon.

SUKAN SPORTS

Throughout my youth, I always dreamed of Sukan Sports as a palatial sports emporium in the heart of leafy Caversham, crammed with attentive sales assistants with gloves and jerseys wall to wall. Sadly this illusion was shattered in the mid 80s when my dad took me on a surprise visit when he was working close by in Reading.

Outwardly, Sukan Sports may not have been the most impressive backstreet corner shop, but inside it was pure goalkeeping heaven. All the stock was stored out the back, and owner Dave Holmes was more than happy for me to try on gloves and jerseys to my heart's content. Tempting posters covered the walls, all featuring keepers advertising the latest gloves, and irresistible catalogues were casually strewn on the counter.

I came away that day with a Brazilian goalkeeper's jersey and a spanking new glovebag,

my obsession ratcheted up yet another notch. At last I'd visited Shangri-La, actually witnessed the mother lode of exotic, almost legendary equipment.

It was Sukan that had first enabled British professional as well as amateur goalies to get their hands in the kind of modern latex gloves that were proving a hit with

continental stoppers such as Sepp Maier.
Back in 1979, West Ham goalie Phil Parkes
had displayed his head for business by
partnering with Dave Holmes in the
specialist goalkeeper mail-order venture
– whilst continuing to play and helping to
popularise gloves.

"I'm the person who answered the phone,"
Dave told *Glove Story* contributor Justin
Bryant. "Good or bad, I was the only person
involved on a day-to-day basis with Sukan
Sports. My fellow director Phil Parkes had
other things to keep him busy."

The work also involved frequent business
trips to Germany, where Dave met with
directors at Reusch and Uhlsport, and got
to personally select gloves and equipment
for the British market. We've already hinted

"Absolutely brilliant, Phil. Fits like a glove."

at the impact of the company's revolutionary adverts in *Shoot!* and *Match*. Another marketing masterstroke was the full-colour catalogue they produced to showcase all the newest gloves, jerseys and other equipment to a salivating following of enthusiastic goalkeepers.

But Sukan Sports was much

previously haphazard system, deciding which pros should get free gloves, which should pay a reduced amount, and who would need to buy retail.

It was a golden 16 years in the history of goalkeeping from 1979 through to December 1995, when Sukan finally closed its doors. "The reason Sukan Sports closed was mainly economic," Holmes says. "Selling goalkeeper products in 1995 was getting harder and harder. We therefore decided we would close down, rather than risk not being financially viable." As Holmes remembers, frequent changes in brand suppliers led to complications in acquiring glove stock, contributing to his concerns.

"Over the 16 years, we had over 15,000 different goalkeepers as customers, and tried to give the best service we could," Holmes recalls. Happily, Dave's contributions did not go unnoticed. In 2014, the FA presented him with a special 'Recognition of Service to Goalkeeping Award,' alongside Ray Clemence, Bob Wilson, Alan Hodgkinson and Mike Kelly.

more than a mail-order shop. It also played a leading role in the development of kit sponsorship. "When I started helping Uhlsport," Dave Holmes explains, "there was no system to record who they supplied gloves to, either under contract or through goodwill, or how much they gave away each season."

His response was to bring order to the

David Holmes
Director

The next time you're poring over internet pages full of new, strange, instantly accessible gloves, remember the part Sukan Sports played in paving the way for the goalkeeper's glove revolution in Britain.

Phil's own photo of the FA Cup, chez Parkes.

The Greatest SAVES

No 7

JOE HART
SLOVENIA 0-0 ENGLAND
Date: 11 October 2016
Venue: Stozice Stadium, Ljubljana

With Gareth Southgate's England in terrible form for this World Cup qualifier and question marks hanging ominously over the head of Torino loanee Joe Hart, the writing seemed to be on the wall from the kick-off.

Disjointed England were clearly never going to score, and the defence were in suicide mode, with Dier and Henderson playing canny throughballs to Slovenian forwards, only to be rescued by Hart.

Panned for his schoolboy errors against Wales and Iceland that finally scuppered England's dysfunctional Euro 2016 campaign, crowbarred out of Manchester by Pep Guardiola and barely third choice England keeper in the eyes of the media, Hart's shattered confidence visibly began to grow.

Moments into the second half, Hart pulled off one of the saves of his career. A bullet corner was glanced into the extreme top left angle of his goal. One second later, Hart lay injured in the back of his net while the ball lay safely in Row Z. You have to watch the slo-mo to see how he leapt to instinctively touch the speeding ball on to his crossbar, then as he crashed painfully into the upright, somehow had the awareness to pat the falling ball away beyond the post

It was a Man of the Match performance where Hart's deserved player rating of 10 was eight higher than any of his hapless team-mates.

A one-man show of true world class.

That's up there with the very best...

GOALS ARE BIG

Do you remember the first time, as a kid, when you got to stand in a full-size goal? The way the posts seemed miles apart, twelve feet away on either side of you, somewhere in the middle-distance. And as for the crossbar, you could forget it, dangling there eight feet up in the air. You tried but failed to jump up and touch it, so the next task was to climb a post or borrow a playmate's shoulders so you could grab hold of the bar and dangle there for a few seconds, looking out at the gigantic penalty-box from the perspective of a proper grown-up goalie.

Goals are big. And, every so often, some publicity-hungry part-time pundit will even wheel out the crowd-pleasing idea of making them even bigger. People are taller than they were in the Victorian age, after all. And everybody likes the idea of seeing games end up 7-6 instead of 2-1.

But goalkeepers prefer goals just the way they are, ta very much. They're definitely big enough. And, on that one-in-a-million occasion when chance throws you a helping hand, making the goal even that tiny bit smaller, it would be wrong not to accept the gift.

Take a bough: Mother Nature lends a helping hand in leafy Leicestershire.

COFFER SPORTS

Coffer Sports were perhaps best known for their football fan-friendly bling back in the medallion-man 70s. They had a wonderful range of pendants, identity bracelets, sew-on patches, lapel badges and key-rings, all tastefully crowned with enamel club badges.

But when it came to sporting cool, Coffer had another string to its bow alongside the iconic Leeds United 'Smiley' necklace. The company also manufactured goalkeepers' gloves, their first product to market being a basic green cotton model

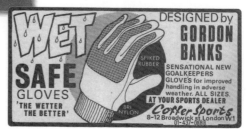

the Wet Safe and International ranges. As you might have expect, the former was a wet-weather glove, with the unique, must-have bonus of being ambidextrous!

Check out a retail price list from 1973 to see how the quality stepped up. Cotton Gloves (boys) were just 45p per pair, with the men's size ranging up to 50p. Meanwhile, Wet Safe Gloves (boys) were £1.30, and International Gloves (boys) £1.95 – or £2.15 for youth/men's size.

Along with caps, jerseys and tracksuits, Coffer's focus on the goalkeeping market was really pushing the envelope. A peaked cap would set you back 58p, or you could go waterproof for just 20p more. A sound investment, we think you'll agree.

In the early 80s, Coffer entered the world

endorsed by Gordon Banks.

'Cotton interlock or snug-round-the-wrist fitting', these babies boasted 'sure-grip rubber on the back to aid punching'. And did we mention that they were 'attractively boxed'?

Next, they went all up-market with

A GORDON BANKS
GOAL KEEPER CAP
ADJUSTABLE SIZE 6⅞-7¼
EMPIRE MADE

his Southampton team-mates all wore Patrick; but alas it wasn't long before this adventurous, innovative company ran into financial troubles in a highly competitive market.

of kit manufacture, producing strips for Swindon Town, Bristol City and Rochdale. Now with Peter Shilton on board, the goalkeepers' range was attractive, effective and much more in sync with their rivals. Shilton may have had a contractual agreement that he could wear a Coffer Sports jersey while

COFFER
SPORTSWEAR

THE GORDON BANKS

Wet Safe

GOALKEEPERS GLOVES

MADE BY COFFER SPORTS   GENTS LARGE

ADIDAS

Technological advances since the advent of the modern latex-palmed glove have mostly been minor. Building on the technology and style of some great gloves endorsed by Ivan Curkovic and Toni Schumacher, improvements were limited to changes in latex formulas and a wider variety of styles and palm cuts. Save for one notable exception: the Adidas Fingersave.

In these revolutionary 90s gloves, firm but flexible plastic spines ran the length of the fingers to the back of the wrist. They were designed to stop the fingers from hyper-extending when saving very hard shots, and proved a massive hit with the buying public.

When we were in Germany recently, visiting Adidas HQ, we spoke to Guenter Pfau who was the company's project manager during this time.

"The patent on the gloves belonged to Endrik Fleischmann," Guenter recalled. "He requested the patent in May 1985 but it wasn't finally issued until February 1994. Endrik had approached other glove companies, Uhlsport

110

and Reusch, who more or less dominated the market at the time. But they weren't willing to take a risk on this glove.

"He then offered the idea to Adidas which remarkably was refused at first. Some time later, in 1994, he contacted my superior and myself because no other company seemed to believe in his concept. At that time I was working on a concept with spines too, but as an inhand. I'd only just started my 'career' as product manager, so I was more open -minded to 'crazy' or different concepts!

"We agreed with Endrik in integrating the glove for Adidas. The selection of the name 'Fingersave' was a result of an internal brainstorming, and as a non-native English-speaking person it was easier for me to create that name. We didn't want to highlight the medical aspect – 'save the finger' – but to highlight the performance idea – 'save the shot'. Fingersave was the result.

"The concept was there but no production plant was able to produce this glove. A guy called Peter Hochmuth and myself first worked with a manufacturing company in Munich but in the end it was Peter's own company that took the risk to produce the spines and the glove. We were late for a coordinated launch of the glove in 1995, but ran a 'soft launch' instead to test different markets and convince more goal-keepers about the idea."

Working without any marketing budget, the result was a word-of-mouth buzz which eventually gave rise to an acknowledged classic.

Saint-Étienne's Ivan Curkovic first endorsed Adidas gloves in the late 70s.

LEFT OR RIGHT?

Here's a question for you. The answer might just influence your thinking the next time you're facing a penalty – and help you to save it.

Q: At which half of the goal should the penalty taker aim to give themselves a statistically proven 98% chance of success (providing they hit the target)?

From a goalie's perspective, should you dive left or right? Based on a huge sample of kicks in recent British and European competition, the answer is... neither!

A: The correct answer is the top half!

That's right. If the penalty taker successfully hits the top half of the goal, there's only a 2% chance of you saving it. That's partly because you always step forward to narrow the angle and then dive out towards one post or the other. Gravity then plays its part, allowing the ball to sail safely into the top half of the net.

See Rob Jovanovic's *Moving the Goalposts* for the whole statistical justification of the fact. The book is full of these astonishing nuggets of information. Meanwhile, consider the cunning sideways skip, or possibly learning to dive upwards?

Brought up on *Football Focus*, I wasn't old enough to see Bob Wilson in action before his retirement from the game in 1974, but getting to meet him was still very special. It's not often that you get to talk to a goalkeeping great about his life in football, let alone spend the afternoon round his house eating cake.

Bob is still as passionate today about the art of goalkeeping as when he was a teenager. Born in Chesterfield, he earned three caps for England Schoolboys before becoming eligible for Scotland in 1970 when qualification was extended.

Ironically, his father didn't let him sign for Manchester United at first – not considering it a proper job – but while training as a teacher at Loughborough, he played for Wolves

reserves, and was sounded out by Arsenal. "Without Arsenal Football Club there would never have been a Bob Wilson," Bob reflects. "I made my first-team debut in 1963, when I was 22, but didn't become first choice until 1968."

Bob ended up making 308 first-team appearances for the Gunners. "My best ever contract at Arsenal was £130 a week plus bonuses – £4 for a win, £2 for a draw – but it was never about the money back then."

Wilson was part of the bare hands and spit generation, only occasionally reaching for a pair of black woollen gloves.

"More to keep the hands warm, to be honest. Then just after the Mexico World Cup I moved on to the green cotton as Gordon Banks had brought out a range. They cost me around 5 shillings a pair! Gloves back then were really ineffective, more a physiological help. It was only on those rainy days and a muddy pitch they were really of any use. I always felt better playing without gloves."

Having appeared as a World Cup pundit in 1970, Bob soon slipped into a 28-year TV career presenting *Football Focus*, then *Grandstand* as well as *Match of the Day*, before moving to ITV. To so many kids growing up at this time, he was the face of Saturday sport on TV, before you headed off to either play or watch a game.

But his media career wasn't enough to prevent Bob returning to Arsenal in 1975.

"When I began, there were no goalkeeping coaches as such. After Terry Neill, the Arsenal managers I worked under were Don Howe, Bruce Rioch, George Graham and Arsène Wenger.

"I prolonged Pat Jennings' career," Bob says proudly. "Got a good nine years out of him; but I never taught him anything. I just offered my enthusiasm! I also coached 'freelance' at Southampton, Watford, Luton and QPR – and even coached Ray Clemence a few times 'under the radar', as a favour to David Pleat."

Furthermore, as we were leafing through Bob's extensive collection of cuttings and photos, we came across a letter from Brian Clough thanking him for his analysis on Hamburg after Nottingham Forest had won the European Cup.

It's hard to argue with Bob's management credentials, though that remains a story of what might have been – a bit like his season spent playing for Melchester Rovers in the mid 80s!

IN GREAT SHAPE
with
⚡*Russell Hall*
Sportswear

FIRST GLOVE

Sébastien Frey

"I was four years of age when I got my first pair of proper gloves. They were from my father, who was a goalkeeper too.
They were a pair of Uhlsport (034) gloves, the style that Dino Zoff used to wear."

The Greatest SAVES

No 8

PETER SHILTON
COVENTRY CITY 0-0 FOREST
Date: 22 April 1978
Venue: Highfield Road

When Forest visited Highfield Road at the end of the 1977/78 season, Brian Clough and Peter Taylor's boys (let's not forget the former Boro keeper!) needed one point to win the First Division title for their first and only time. Playing it cagily, the pressure began to tell. The best chance of the whole game – a sitting-duck certainty from just four yards out – came from a right-wing cross from Ian Wallace which looped right on to the head of Sky Blues centre-forward Mick Ferguson. Unmarked, he powered it straight at the empty goal.

Enter Peter Shilton from nowhere, sprinting furiously along his goal-line to batter the ball away to safety. Ferguson's astonished reaction said it all.

Interestingly, Shilts' own pick of his greatest saves came against Scotland, and a long shot from Kenny Dalglish. Diving for the ball with his left hand, at the last microsecond he pulled his right arm over and pushed it away in amazing style.

The image appears on the cover of *Peter Shilton: The Autobiography*.

It looked a certain goal...

PETER SHILTON

JUST KEEPERS

Back in 1996, when Just Keepers first opened for business in Hinckley, Leicestershire, goalkeeper gloves were surprisingly still hard to come by. General sports shops were reluctant to stock the high-end, quality brands that goalies were crying out for. What the world really needed was a specialist goalkeeper store...

As if by magic, Just Keepers was born – and has since sold close to a million pairs of gloves over the years. "And remember the gloves are sent out all over the world,"

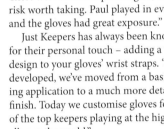

the boys behind the brand told us. "We've shipped to over 45 countries in the last few months alone.

"As for our best-selling gloves, one of them was the Nike Tiempo Premier World Cup Special in 2006, which were worn exclusively by Paul Robinson..." Just Keepers took a big risk at the time, as they were offered exclusivity by Nike to sell the glove in the lead-up to the tournament and committed to thousands of units. "We were praying that Paul would be fully fit for the tournament!

There were a few sleepless nights, but it was a risk worth taking. Paul played in every game and the gloves had great exposure."

Just Keepers has always been known for their personal touch – adding a unique design to your gloves' wrist straps. "As we've developed, we've moved from a basic printing application to a much more detailed finish. Today we customise gloves for many of the top keepers playing at the highest level all over the world."

It's Peter Schmeichel: give him a big hand.

BOOK KEEPING

"Goalkeeping may appear on the surface to be a rather uninteresting and vague topic upon which to base a book. But, in fact, the subject of the goalkeeper comprises not only interesting material and information but also it can become a subject to which in certain respects there is no ending and no answer." – Bob Wilson, *Goalkeeping* (Pelham Books, 1970).

"In my teens there were few coaching books, and in those that existed, there was little information about goalkeeping. There were no goalkeeping coaches, and team trainers found keepers 'a bit of a nuisance.' After I had joined the professional ranks I would go back to the clubhouse each afternoon to seek extra training. Most times our coach would say, 'Why don't you go home and have a rest?' Or the equipment manager would suggest, as I bugged him for extra training kit, 'Why don't you go and have a game of golf?'" – Tony Waiters, *Coaching the Goalkeeper* (World of Soccer, 1992).

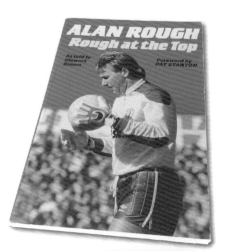

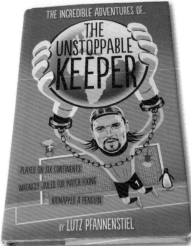

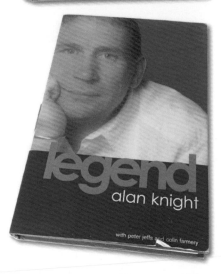

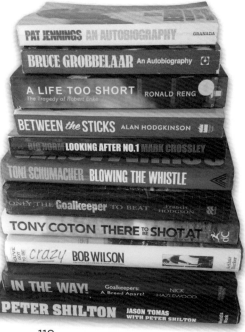

NORMAN 'BLACK JAKE' UPRICHARD

WITH CHRIS WESTCOTT
FOREWORD BY HARRY GREGG

Did You Know? Norman got his nickname after travelling to a match in the back of a coal lorry.

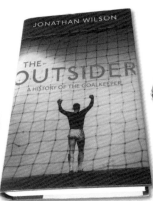

JONATHAN WILSON

THE OUTSIDER

A HISTORY OF THE GOALKEEPER

banksy
my autobiography

gordon banks

THE AUTOBIOGRAPHY

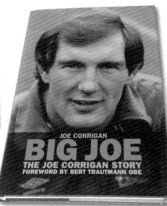

JOE CORRIGAN

BIG JOE

THE JOE CORRIGAN STORY
FOREWORD BY BERT TRAUTMANN OBE

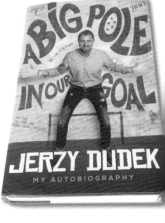

A BIG POLE IN OUR GOAL

JERZY DUDEK
MY AUTOBIOGRAPHY

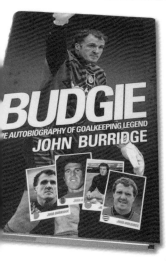

BUDGIE

THE AUTOBIOGRAPHY OF GOALKEEPING LEGEND
JOHN BURRIDGE

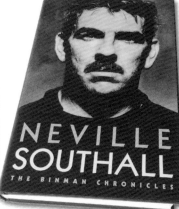

NEVILLE SOUTHALL
THE BINMAN CHRONICLES

IN THE FIRING LINE

THE JIM LEIGHTON STORY

Jim Leighton and
Ken Robertson

MY HERO

On Twitter and the Got, Not Got blog we asked you to send in treasured snaps of you in your younger days meeting your goalkeeping heroes.

We had a fantastic response.

Here's the best of the bunch, mostly taken long before the age of the selfie..

120

Gary Bailey signs for Mark Partington. David Pallister meets Pavel Srnicek and Shaka Hislop. Pete Weller and Neville Southall.

Facing page: Mark Taylor "My dad organised the Hitachi sponsorship and we received our kit from Ray Clemence." Matt Freeman and Bruce Grobbelaar. Steve Hale with Peter Bonetti. Two Pats, Nash and Jennings, Matt Lumb meets Dave Watson.

Joe Corrigan is cornered by Gary Foy and cousins, Graham and Kit. Dylan O'Connor meets Shay Given. Paul Owens, in the middle of Alan Fettis's defensive wall. Dale Walker with Eddie Niedzwiecki.

Legends on the line No 8 David Seaman

David Seaman is a true colossus of English goalkeeping. With a career spanning 1982-2004 and a safe hand in so many massive League and international games, it's hard to know where to start questioning the affable Yorkshireman. So many aspects of his career and personality have already been sounded out, endlessly analysed, even mythologised...

Those penalty saves for England in Euro '96 stand out as moments seared into many fans' memories. The quarter-final save from Spain's Nadal was widely celebrated, but it was somehow trumped in tabloid terms by the stop from Scotland's Gary McAllister, where Uri Geller claimed he moved the ball telepathically.

We could always ask him about fishing. But when it comes to headline scoops, we'd never beat the hard-hitting TV documentary that saw Joe Pasquale controversially expose Seaman's Tackle, David's personally endorsed angling gear, as a load of old cod.

Then there's the iconic ponytail. But what could we possibly add to the shock revelation, in an interview with comedian Lenny Sherman, that Seaman still keeps it in a drawer in his bedroom?

Let's kick off by asking him how come

he ended up in goal instead of shooting for glory as a big number 9? He can't possibly have been asked that one before.

"I always loved the positive response and praise I received when I played in goal for my school team," David replies. "I seemed to have a natural talent for the position," he points out the obvious, ever so gently. "And of course it helped that I was always very tall for my age."

What about if you had a chance to play in one game again. Which would you choose?

"If I could play one game over again it would be my first game in the World Cup finals. It was France '98 and we played against Tunisia in the Stade Vélodrome in Marseille. I felt so proud to be playing for my country in the World Cup. It proved to me that dreams can come true."

Of course, we've always got our specialist question about favourite gloves!

"Once I became England's number 1, all my gloves were made to measure and I was sponsored by various companies over the span of my career. I enjoyed the majority of my successes wearing Reusch, Adidas, Umbro and Puma."

During Euro '96 you wore a pair of fleece-lined Reusch Pro Arrow. Given how warm it was that summer, why the fleecy pair?

"I liked the fleece-lined Reusch gloves because they were very comfortable. The first time I tried them on I couldn't believe how great they felt on my hands and after trying them in training I was also impressed with their performance. Given the successes that we achieved in the Euro '96 tournament, I'd say they were a perfect choice."

You've said in the past that your save from Stoke's Paul Peschisolido was probably one of the greatest of your career. But was there any other that you'd put on par with that? When you were at QPR there was one from John

Barnes that featured on the classic *Saves Galore* video...

"I did make a real split-second reaction save against John Barnes while playing at QPR, but the Paul Peschi-solido is by far my best save ever. Why? Because it included a very quick change of direction, and total control at full stretch."

The fleeting image of David Seaman as a blurred superhero finally provides us with a question we're pretty sure he's never been asked before.

What would you do if you were invisible for a day...?

adidas

David Seaman
Arsenal & England

DAVID
SEAMAN

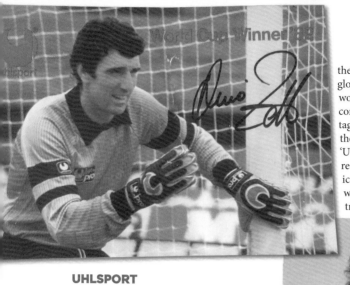

World Cup Winner '82

the market leaders, with their gloves worn by many of the world's top professionals. The company had a distinct advantage over many of their rivals: their logo. The highly stylised 'U' was at once instantly recognisable and immediately iconic. It certainly didn't hurt when Dino Zoff lifted the trophy at the 1982 World Cup

UHLSPORT

As latex goalkeeper gloves slowly grew in popularity in the 1970s, sports equipment companies began to recognise the possibilities of the new market. Among the first (and best) to exploit it was Uhlsport.

Founded in 1948 in Germany by Karl Uhl, Uhlsport at first made only leather studs for football boots. Over the next few decades they expanded and began producing boot soles, shin pads, and, of course, goalkeeper gloves.

From the beginning of the latex glove era, Uhlsport became one of

Kodachrome TRANSPARENCY

PROCESSED BY Kodak

wearing his Uhlsport gloves for all the world to see.

Uhlsport became an immediate hit in Britain in the 1980s, worn by many of the era's top goalkeepers, including Peter Shilton, Jimmy Rimmer, John Lukic, Neville Southall and many more. Under contract to a different company at the time of the 1980 FA Cup final, Phil Parkes

Did You Know?
'Hand shoe' is German for 'glove'.

TORWART-HANDSCHUHE
GOALKEEPERS GLOVES
GANTS DE GARDIEN DE BUT
GUANTI DA PORTIERE

uhlsport
MADE BY UHLSPORT

wore a pair of Uhlsport gloves 'doctored' to look like his sponsor brand, because the Uhlsports were so much better! High-profile international keepers such as Zoff, Colombia's René Higuita, Belgium's Michel Preud'Homme, and West Germany's Bodo Ilgner ensured the brand remained highly visible on the world stage.

In the early 1990s, amid fierce competition from German rivals Reusch and UK upstarts Sondico – not to mention sportswear giant Adidas – Uhlsport developed their wildly popular APG (Adhesive Power Grip) latex. Today the gloves remain as popular as ever, worn by the likes of France and Tottenham star Hugo Lloris, as well as numerous

Bryan Gunn
Norwich City

goalkeepers during the 2016 Euros.

In recent years, Uhlsport even released a line of retro replicas of some of their most loved models. Once again the company demonstrated the way they embrace their proud history, even as they continue to look forward.

125

TABLE TOP KEEPERS - PART 2

Thanks go out to Paul Woozley for giving us the lowdown on the unique foibles of oldfootballgames.co.uk's historic collection.

F.C. Rapid fussball (main picture) - 1950s German game complete with disco-dancing keeper, who just happens to be three times taller than his goal.

International Table Football (top left) – A goalie with a strange 'lobster' suntan is augmented by unexpected sound effects, a rendition of 'Olé, olé, we are the fans' being provided via electronic wizardry.

Dua-Soc (bottom left) A pre-war game where the players are actually made from curtain rail ends. Not having any arms or means of movement could be considered disadvantages for a keeper.

Five-a-Side (right page, top left) Made by Pepys, more famously known for the Penalty! card game. The lead cast goalkeeper exudes class and elegance in his pose and demeanour, a gentleman footballer.

TopScor (continuing clockwise) 'True-to-life mechanical men' star in this Spears game – decently posed in front of a tiny goal (nil-nil anyone?) with the obligatory metal rod up his behind!

Hot Shot A 70s gem from Tri-ang featuring high-quality goal, oversize linen shorts and a magnificent target practice board. The players were created so you could control their shots to target the various holes.

Kika-Goal! The original 1950s version of Striker featured 'diving goalkeepers' with fab articulated control rods. Sadly the design only lets the keeper dive forwards, perfect to recreate the mad Hugo Lloris dash from your goal-line.

Team Football French, Striker-ish game featuring the push-down head mechanism, plus tiny goalkeeper control rod and arms that can be manually positioned – perfect for the 'one for the cameras' flying save pose.
Girl-Kick A German 80s knock-off of the classic Tipp Kick game that is billed as 'Die Party-Sensation', no less. Scantily clad female players are actually extremely well designed and work brilliantly!

MUD

Wouldn't it be great to see some of today's top goalies play in the same winter conditions that we have to endure – or used to? How would they fare in the muddy penalty areas of 20 or 30 years ago, which are still par for the course in school and park football?

It's years since many Prem goalies even got their knees muddy, having been plucked from the reality of churned-up goal areas into the pristine emerald swards of Academy grounds aged seven. Today there are

Moment in the sun: John Connaughton only played three games for Man United, but later appeared 218 times for Port Vale

imported PL keepers who have never seen a puddle on a pitch, let alone known the joy of soaring headlong into a soft, slippery, chill mudbath.

How refreshing to hear that West Ham's Joe Hart has had the back lawn of his Essex mansion replaced with good old-fashioned mud. Goalie mates Peter Cech (Arsenal) and Charlie Grainger (Orient) often join him for an evening reliving their misspent youth.

GIANLUIGI BUFFON
ITALY 1-1 ROMANIA
Date: 13 June 2008
Venue: Letzigrund, Zurich

It was a penalty kick which, by rights, should have sent Italy crashing out of the 2008 European Championships at the group stage.

The score stood one apiece in the 81st minute when Romanian goalscorer Adrian Mutu smacked his spot-kick goalward, apparently giving Italian goalkeeper and captain Buffon no chance.

A wonderful *Evening Standard* match report describes what happened next in near mystical terms – "Mutu, it seemed, had scored, given that the ball had been hit down the middle and Buffon had opted to dive left. Somehow, from somewhere, Buffon suddenly discovered the ability to suspend himself in mid-air – in much the same way Michael Jordan once did above a basketball hoop; in much the same way, without wishing to sound too ridiculous, they do in those *Matrix* movies. It enabled the giant of a goalkeeper to first get his right glove, then his right boot to the ball and make a save that was simply breathtaking in its execution."

It looked like curtains for Italy...

Poland

Tomaszewski

World Cup Appearances	7
World Cup Goals	0
International Appearances	56
International Goals	0
Height	6' 1"

Italy

Dino Zoff

World Cup Appearances	3
World Cup Goals	0
International Appearances	61
International Goals	0
Height	5'9½"

Manchester City

Joe Corrigan

International Goals	0
International Appearances	7
League Goals	0
League Appearances	412
Height	6'4½"

TOP TRUMPS

Do you remember the old playground favourite, Top Trumps? Dubreq's multi-themed card game was introduced in the UK in the mid 70s, based on a popular European forerunner, and survived well into the 90s. Long since bought out, the brand survives to this day, as well as living on in the competitive stats that now often appear on the front of football cards.

In the football version of the game, the goalies always tended to be useful in certain categories – height, obviously; League and international appearances – even if they did prove less than deadly in the goalscoring stakes.

During our extensive original research for GLOVE STORY – in the pub reminiscing about the 80s – one sage professor of pop-cultural studies happened to mention a legendary Top Trumps card for Norwich City, Rangers and England keeper, Chris Woods.

Sure enough, a moment's Googling confirmed the unbelievable existence of the worst Top Trumps card in history:

International Goals: 0
International Appearances: 0
League Goals: 0
League Appearances: 0
Height: 5'2".

Just joking. Young Chris was actually 6'0", but you do take the point that this card wasn't exactly the ace in the pack. However, it turned out that Chris would have the last laugh. Not only did he go on to play 43 times for his country and make almost 600 League appearances in a 20-year career. It also turned out the card was in a rare vintage Forest-only set that would have cost us £25 on eBay.

So you'll just have to imagine it!

Great Big Joe: never knowingly beaten for height.

West Germany

Sepp Maier

World Cup Appearances	12
World Cup Goals	0
International Appearances	79
International Goals	0
Height	6' 0"

Liverpool

Ray Clemence

International Appearances	32
International Goals	0
League Appearances	361
League Goals	0
Height	5'11½"

131

David James stands apart from most of the legendary goalkeepers featured in the book, chiefly because his talents always ran to much more than keeping the ball out of the net.

A furiously modern Renaissance Man, James was once a school record holder in the high jump, a noted collector of Chopper bikes, a master of the decks (well, DJ DJ does have a certain ring to it), and even artist extraordinaire, having found time to illustrate a children's book. Let's see – that was somewhere in-between modelling for Armani in his underpants and trialling for the Miami Dolphins as a specialist goal kicker.

brand known to man, from being an early Puma endorsee with his own range of gloves to Sondico's pin-up boy.

When we met up with David recently for an afternoon of talking goalkeeping, we got on to the subject of his habit of creatively redesigning his own gloves. Not content with the standard pair out the packet, David would take out the Sharpie and give them a complete makeover. Inspirational phrases such as *'numquam dubitatio'* (Latin for 'never doubt') would be etched into the palms or straps.

Even on the eve of Wayne Rooney's debut against Australia at Upton Park, he sat and reworked a brand new Umbro pair. A Roy Lichtenstein-inspired drawing of Michael Owen appeared on the left glove, while the right was inscribed with the words 'Sweet As', in reference to the lady in his life.

"I'll tell you what," he said. "I'll dig them out when I get home and will send you a photo." And, true to his word, he did just that.

At the age of 15 he was told by the English high jump coach that within 3 years he'd be British champion. Instead he opted for the lure of £27.50 a week at Watford on the government's Youth Training Scheme. The decision must have come as a relief to the goalkeeper glove industry, as David has since been known to use practically every

SELLS

Adam sells goalkeeper products. Adam Sells, that is – of Sells Goalkeeper Products. We asked Adam how we might ourselves set about becoming goalie glove barons. About beginnings and high points. And about nominative determinism...

"I began working initially for a French brand, BGB, and then set up Selsport," he told us. "Sells Goalkeeper Products was formed on the last day of 2001. Although I shared a huge passion for goalkeeping, having played and coached in professional football, it all happened by accident.

"We set up a small range of around 11 adult gloves and three junior versions. I felt there was an opportunity to establish a 'goalkeeper only' brand in the marketplace, using the very best materials to create the ultimate in goalkeeper products.

"I wanted the brand to be specialist, to design and develop product that perhaps the general sport brands wouldn't have the time or resources to build and manufacture. I felt specialist keepers would identify with a product line of gloves, apparel and accessories that went the extra mile. Now, many years later, the technology has advanced but the values are just the same.

We continue to push boundaries. "The Sells gloves were first worn in a professional game by Charlton Athletic's Dean Kiely against Middlesbrough at the Riverside Stadium in a Premier League fixture on 2 February, 2002. The model used was the 'Adhesion Plus Wrap' which was predominately white with a roll finger cut, and this look and styling has become synonymous with the brand. Dean was one of the original shareholders and remains both a great personal friend and ambassador for the brand.

"On the wall in our showroom, we have a giant version of that glove together with an image of Dean in that very first game in which the SGP logo featured.

"The highlight, and without question the brand's finest hour, came on the 25th May 2005 in Istanbul when Liverpool keeper Jerzy Dudek lifted the UEFA Champions League trophy following a dramatic penalty shoot-out.

"I was lucky enough to be in Turkey for that memorable evening and felt an immense amount of pride, seeing the fledgling brand achieve the ultimate in club football."

Red Jerzy: Dudek does wonders for Sells sales.

133

EXPLOSION IN A PAINT FACTORY

Green was still the dominant goalkeeping colour in England in 1991-92 but changes were afoot, escalated by an outside influence.

When the new Premier League kicked off in August 1992, match officials were now to be seen in green shirts with black pinstripes. While nowadays the officials are last in the kit priority order (behind home outfield, away outfield, home GK and away GK), back then it meant that, overnight, netminders had to find different colours.

Coupled with this was a greater sense of adventure from the manufacturers, emboldened as each new design development manifested itself. Received wisdom was that the garishness served a purpose in distracting inrushing forwards, though a scientific study proving that remains elusive.

Coloured blobs quickly became very common along with abstract patterns which represented everything and nothing. Take, for example, the alternative jersey which Sheffield Wednesday's Chris Woods and Kevin Pressman wore from 1993-95 – a mix of the club's initials as well as aggressive Puma branding, all topped off in a purple, peach and green colour scheme.

The mainly red outfit David Seaman wore

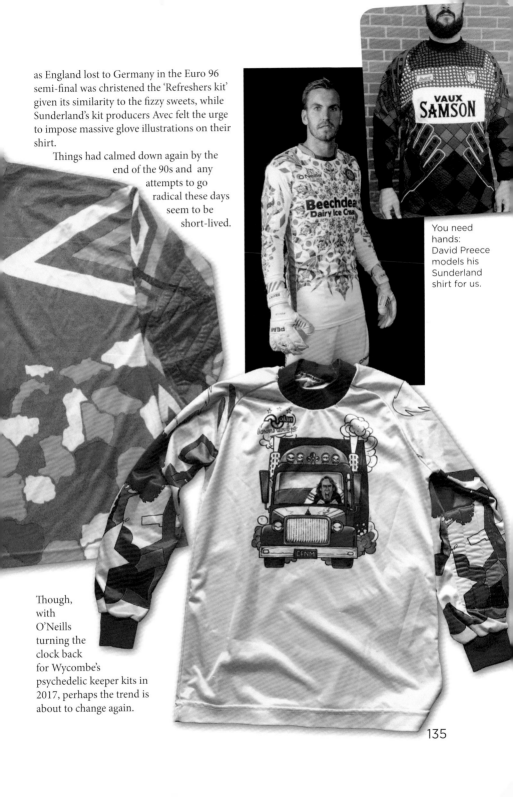

as England lost to Germany in the Euro 96 semi-final was christened the 'Refreshers kit' given its similarity to the fizzy sweets, while Sunderland's kit producers Avec felt the urge to impose massive glove illustrations on their shirt.

Things had calmed down again by the end of the 90s and any attempts to go radical these days seem to be short-lived.

You need hands: David Preece models his Sunderland shirt for us.

Though, with O'Neills turning the clock back for Wycombe's psychedelic keeper kits in 2017, perhaps the trend is about to change again.

135

COMPETITION WINNERS

Today you can enter a prize competition simply by texting 'yes' on your phone, but times used to be so very different. Magazines such as *Shoot!* and *Match* were littered each week with tantalising prizes ranging from days out with your footballing hero, to winning the shirt off his back – all for completing a quiz, answering a tie-break question and pestering your mum for an 8p stamp.

A few weeks later you'd be desperately scouring the 'Winners Announced' section. It was the same when you entered TV competitions on programmes such as *Swap Shop*, except they'd pull the lucky winner's postcard out of a bulging mailbag live on air.

One week, I entered a competition to win Ray Clemence's Admiral England jersey on *Saturday Superstore*, hosted by Mike Read – and so, of course, did my close mate and teenage goalkeeping rival, Neil Smithard. The show had a special feature about goalkeepers' gloves where David Icke asked Ray to try on various pairs. What happened the following week proved that dreams really can come true (for other people). *Superstore* guest Bob Carolgees lowered Spit the Dog down to the postbag, and the puppet emerged with a postcard in his muzzle.

I was gutted and green with

envy when Bob read out Neil's name. The shirt I'd so badly wanted to win was now going to be living just a few streets away. We met up that week for training, and Neil was actually wearing it. I'll never know how I managed to offer my congratulations without ripping it off his back.

"I remember sitting on the sofa when Spit pulled out the postcard," Neil still recalls that fateful morning so much more happily than me. "I could clearly see an image of *HMS Victory* on it and I knew straight away it was my card. Still, when he read out my name to confirm I'd won I started running round the lounge like a kid possessed. I'd never won anything before and this was one special prize. I still have the shirt to this day and it hangs proudly in my wardrobe!"

My own lucky day finally arrived 12 years later, when a Sukan Sports leaflet offered customers the chance to win a boxful of Uhslport goodies signed by Tim Flowers. The only snag was, you had to correctly guess the glove sizes of 10 of Uhlsport's Football League keepers. How the heck was I going to get all those right?

Luckily, however, my

Glittering prize: Ray Clemence's actual, actual England shirt.

mate John Williams happened to be married to the sister of then-Norwich player Rob Newman. A series of underhand phone calls later, Rob was cued to ask Canaries keeper Bryan Gunn for his glove size... and did he by any chance know the other nine?

A week passed before the phone rang and John supplied all the answers that Bryan

Sūkan Sports 2 Piggotts Road, Caversham
Reading, Berkshire. RG4 8EN
Tel: Reading (01734) 481586

20th March 1995

We would like to thank everybody who took the trouble to complete and return the questionnaires we sent out in November 1994.

The competition to guess goalkeepers glove sizes seemed to generate a great deal of interest, Bryan Gunn informs us that he even had some people contact him to request his glove size, and the size of others on the list!

The winner was Robbie Stokes from Portsmouth, and the runners-up were Steve Hale from Swindon, Daniel Tate from Bedford and Mark Hancock from Bristol.

The correct answers were: size eight and a half (Jon Hallworth), size nine (Fraser Ligby, Ian Walker), size nine and a half (Jürgen Sommer), size ten (Tim Flowers, Bryan Gunn, Alan Kelly, John Lukic, Gordon Marshall), size eleven (Mike Hooper).

NEW FOR 1995

with the kind co-operation of uhlsport we are able to offer for a limited period the new 107 gloves that

Gunn had kindly found out from that lengthy list of doubtless slightly confused keepers.

Cheating, you reckon? I still prefer to think of it as creative thinking...

The 80s, perfectly summed up in one photo.

137

Peter Bonetti is perhaps best remembered for his outstanding performance in the dramatic 1970 FA Cup final and replay, when he almost single-handedly kept glamour boys Chelsea in the game against Don Revie's Leeds United. There's also the little matter of his being a goalkeeping glove revolutionary; but first let's focus on Bonetti's part in that classic final.

"Everything that was good about Peter's goalkeeping, and that amounted to a great deal, was on show at Wembley and Old Trafford," Bob Wilson said of Bonetti, in *You've Got to Be Crazy.* "Wembley was as much a story of Eddie Gray versus Peter Bonetti as Leeds against Chelsea. Gray was at his exhilarating best but Bonetti matched everything the Scottish international threw at him. The first game ended 2-2 but in the replay Chelsea won 2-1. How they did it against the best team in the country, and with their keeper crippled, remains a mystery."

We did say Bonetti's defensive ramparts were erected almost single-handedly.

Well, his efforts were heroically single-legged, too, throughout the replay and extra-time. "Bonetti played most of the game hobbling on one leg after an unsavoury challenge by Mick Jones. His left knee, badly damaged, became very swollen. Taking off from the left leg was impossible, and it cost Chelsea the opening goal of the game, scored by Jones.

"The turning point though was when, with the score 1-1, the courageous Bonetti made two great saves from Terry Cooper. Peter 'The Cat' Bonetti had saved Chelsea again, something which their fans had come to expect from the slim five feet ten and a half keeper, who made up for his lack of height with a Continental-style agility.

"The final reports referred to Peter as 'world-class', ironic words bearing in mind what happened to him a few weeks later in Mexico..."

As Wilson hints, Bonetti's great one-club career was dented by just one of his seven England appearances – the 1970 World Cup match "in which

THE PETER BONETTI
⚅ METRIC ⚅   ⚅ METRIC ⚅
GOALKEEPERS' GLOVES

Peter
Bonetti's
story

CHELSEA

Testimonial Season 1970/71 Price Three Shillings

England lost their title of world champions."

On a more characteristically upbeat note, Bonetti is untouchable in many ex-keepers' eyes after becoming only the second English endorsee (after Ron Springett) of his own range of gloves. The 'green cotton gloves' venture started in 1968, and it's interesting to note an article in *Goal* magazine from August of that year which confirms a cool 13,000 pairs sold to date. Mind you, we're not so sure about the feature whereby you could "turn the gloves inside-out when they get muddy"!

Bonetti later brought out the iconic 'B' range around 1978/79, several different styles all boasting gripping aids that recalled the humble table tennis bat. It doesn't exactly speak volumes for Peter's confidence in his own line of products that he continued to play bare handed!

Just in case there's any doubt about the quality of the goalkeeper who played 600 League matches for Chelsea, once being voted their greatest ever player, we'll pass on the last word to an expert in the field.

"The three greatest goalkeepers I have ever seen are Gordon Banks, Lev Yashin and Peter Bonetti."

Anyone want to take issue with Pele?

FIRST GLOVE

Martyn Margetson
"My first pair of latex gloves were a black pair of Uhlsport, with a huge white logo on the back, and a red latex palm. My father got them for me, but told me to ignore the guarantee. It said, due to the nature of latex, we can only guarantee the palm for an average of four games! "They are to last the season," were my dad's instructions. I must have been around 13 or 14 years old."

The Greatest SAVES No 10

PETER SCHMEICHEL
RAPID VIENNA 0-2 MAN UNITED
DATE: 4 December 1996
VENUE: Ernst Happel Stadion

It's the Champions' League group stage of 1996/97, and Manchester United are falling under the cosh away at Rapid Vienna. A free kick swings into the box from Schmeichel's left, straight over the top to the other wing.

And now over to Brian Moore in the commentary box, along with excitable cohort Ron Atkinson.

Brian: "Ratajczyk, the Pole. He's crossed it again, and a good one. And nodded down... a *wonderful* save by Schmeichel."

Big Ron: "Brian, that might be..."

Brian: "You won't find a better save anywhere than that. It was past him and he got it away."

Big Ron: "I'm telling you that could be another one of, er, Gordon Banks job. That is an un-be-*lie*-vable save. I shouted 'goal' there. And not only that, he's knocked it away from the danger zone."

Not only had the Dane perfected the skill of leaping downwards to his right far faster than mere gravity allowed, he'd also had the split-second presence of mind to schmite the spinning ball up and over the far post.

A wonderful save by Schmeichel...

BEWARE THE SEVEN BLUNDERS OF THE WORLD

Our homage to goalkeeping draws to an end, but before you go on your way, we warn you to be wary of the pitfalls that can lie in wait...

The Pickpocket

Keep an eye out for ne'er-do-wells lurking behind you, awaiting an opportunity. Newcastle's Shay Given didn't, when he dropped the ball on the turf before preparing to hoof it upfield. Dion Dublin of Coventry snuck up from behind and prodded it into an empty net. An even cheekier version of this saw Gary Crosby nodding the ball out of Andy Dibble's hand as he wound up for a drop-kick, putting Forest 1-0 up against Manchester City.

The Devious Divot

There you are, stooped in preparation to safely gather a daisy-cutter, and suddenly, oops, it hits a divot and loops up over your shoulder, making you look a proper Charlie. Tim Flowers of Blackburn and Tottenham's Ian Walker both suffered this indignity, though on both occasions it would appear to have been a self-inflicted wound, as they had studded up the turf themselves in the days when DIY pitch-markings were allowed.

The Evil Eel

Sometimes the damn ball is like an eel smothered in baby oil. It wriggles and jumps and startles you. Forest's Mark Crossley seemed to have done the hard part, saving a thumping header from Colin Hendry of Blackburn. Both hands pinned the ball to the turf. But it then developed a life of its own, leaping free over his body and over the line. The Premier League's first ever own-goal.

The Air Shot

As the ball trundles your way, you can already picture it sailing heavenwards after a hefty whack upfield. Back in reality, your boot has connected with fresh air and the ball is nestling in the net. Norwich's Bryan Gunn set up to welly a backpass from Rob Ullathorne beyond the far horizon, but missed it and could only watch as it rolled into the net. To make matters worse, this was against Ipswich.

The Ghost

Be warned that the ball can acquire phantom-like properties and pass right through you. Scottish goalies were ever the butt of jokes, so revenge was sweet when Ray Clemence allowed a shot from Kenny Dalglish to pass through his arms and legs at Hampden Park in 1976. Twenty-three years later Manchester United's Massimo Taibi appeared to have a shot from Southampton's Matt Le Tissier covered, when it passed through his grasp, under his body, and between his thighs before rolling slowly over the line.

The Gift

The keeper's sorrow is that having claimed possession of the ball you then have to give it to someone else. But it's always best if that someone else is a team-mate. A goal-kick from Manchester United's Fabien Barthez only travelled 20 yards before finding Thierry Henry with pinpoint accuracy. Henry wasted no time in slotting it past him.

The Turncoat Post

When the very goal that you're defending betrays you. You dive for a shot, it hits the post, rebounds off the back of your head and into the net. Richard Wright, for England against Malta, is among the goalies asking the reasonable question, "What the hell could I do about that?"

AUTHORS

Rob Stokes played in goal for Southern League Waterlooville from 1989-98, making 334 appearances and scoring 2 goals (both penalties!). Rob is a passionate collector of goalkeeping memorabilia, with vintage gloves stretching back to the early 70s. He has a loyal following on Instagram and Twitter. Derek Hammond and Gary Silke are the authors of Got, Not Got, runner-up in the BSBA Football Book of the Year 2012, and the following series of books.

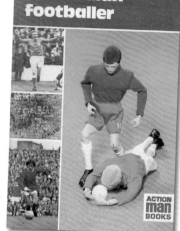

PICTURE CREDITS

Neville Chadwick Photography – chadwicksphoto.co.uk: Shilton on cover; 62; Shilton 86; 92; 128. Simon Mooney: Peter Schmeichel glove on cover; Reusch glovebag 24; Schmeichel gloves 56; Nike gloves 117. Pete Blackman (@peteblackman): Neville Southall figure on cover; glovebags 22/23; Schmeichel model 34; Subbuteo Burridge 79; 83; Seaman model 123; gloves in net 125; 142; back cover. Doug Nash: endpapers and goalie graphics throughout. Andrew Ormerod: quilted shirt on cover; shirt page 14; 80; Bob Wilson 90. Derek Lewens: Jack Kelsey card 6. Dave Holmes: S glove photos 12; Martin Thomas and Eddie Niedzwiecki 15; gloves ad 16; Sukan glovebag 22; contact sheet 23; Schick advert 98; all items on pages 102/103/104; Coffer catalogue 109; Uhlsport factory slides 124. Paul Owens: 13. Jonathon Wheatley: Leeds shirt 15; England shirt 87. Frances Hammond: special thanks for the original artwork 16. Bob Wilson: thanks for the postcard 17; catalogue and school photo page 84/85; Russell Hall catalogue 115; David Seaman 123. Martin Thomas: boots 21; Ron Springett gloves 52; Coffer gloves 108/109; England shirt 134. Peter Mellor: thanks for the hands 25; 76/77. Rebellion Publishing: 'Goalkeeper' and 'Rick Stewart' strips from Roy of the Rovers 30/31. Roy of the Rovers™ is used as a trademark, © Rebellion Publishing. Used with the permission of Rebellion Publishing, 2017. Dave Morcom: 35; Mike Walker 37; 50; Eric Nixon 92; 112. Paul Woozley: games 38/39 and 126/127. Mick Richards: white gloves 52. Falk Siemering: Reusch slides 57. kstudio/Freepik: film strip 59. Simon Kimber: 64. Lee Herring: Ray Clemence Sondico Sports Card 74. Paul Higgs: Sondico Membership Card 75. John Burridge: photo holding shirt 78. Andy Hall: glove and card 79. Lenny Sherman: sweatshirt and kid 85. Trevor Saunders: Kevin Keelan shirt 87. Dave Beasant: portrait and gloves 100. adidas, 3-Bars, 3-Stripes, Brandmark and Trefoil are registered trade marks of the adidas Group, used with permission. Simon Shakeshaft and James Elkin, The Arsenal Shirt Book: shirt 114. David James: gloves 132. Adam Sells: photos 133. Andy @ScotsFootyCards. Pink Southall Umbro shirt 134. David Preece: 'hands' shirt 135. Jesee Rabbeljee: Montoya shirt 135. Neil Smithard: Ray Clemence shirt 137. BBC/Getty Images: licence acquired for still of Ray Clemence and David Icke 137. Alfie Adams: youth 143. Colin Murrant: veteran 143.

ACKNOWLEDGMENTS

All of the goalkeeping gloves, kit, ephemera and memorabilia is from Rob Stokes' personal collection unless otherwise stated.

Thanks to Glove Story illustrator Doug Nash: you can find more of Doug's fantastic goalie graphics at TheArtOfGoalkeeping.com, where they're available as posters and T-shirts.

Follow Doug on Twitter @DougNash9.

Thanks to photographer Pete Blackman (@peteblackman) for all his wonderful photos which appear throughout the book.

Thanks to all the writers who have contributed to the book: David Preece @davidpreece12 ('Premier League Invasion'); Justin Bryant @Keepers_Union ('Jimmy Rimmer', 'Reusch', 'Sondico Sports' and 'Uhlsport'); Neil Andrews @goalkeepersdiff & GoalkeepersAreDifferent.com ('Half Man Half Biscuit' and 'Keepers of the Silver Screen'); Denis Hurley @MuseumOfJerseys & MuseumOfJerseys.com ('Goalie Shirt Evolution' and 'Explosion in a Paint Factory').

Dave Holmes: Thanks for all the photos, information and time poured into this book. You can read more about Sukan Sports at TheGlovebag.com. Paul Woozley: There's loads more fantastic vintage toys where these came from, at OldFootballGames.co.uk. Andrew Ormerod: For more great pics and eccentric stories from the lower reaches of the football pyramid, visit Andy's blog at hoppingaroundhampshire.blogspot.co.uk. Thanks to Martin Thomas, to Ian Milne at Just Keepers, to Adam Sells at Sells Goalkeeping Products and to Kevin Ghartey at Getty Images. The cereal boxes on page 90 were purchased from www.cerealoffers.com. A big thank-you to all of our Kids in Kits: Paul Higgs in the chequered top; Neil Parkins lifting trophy; Mark Allen under the crossbar; Ian Trickett in Sharp kit with hands in air; Matt Howarth holding trophy; Simon Mooney with Uncle in the 70s; Mark Chilab by the flower beds; Mick Richards black-and-white 60s; Rob Richards with balls and trophies; Lloyd Griffith arms outstretched.

Special thanks to all the goalkeepers who have contributed to Glove Story: Bob Wilson, John Burridge, David Seaman, Jordan Pickford, Henrique Hilario, Thibaut Courtois, Martyn Margetson, Peter Hucker, Simon Farnworth, Alan Miller, Sebastian Frey, Jack Butland, Bryan Gunn, David James, Peter Mellor, Dave Beasant, Neville Southall, Wayne Hennessey and Gordon Banks. Alan Knight and the groundstaff at Portsmouth FC for the morning of photography at Fratton Park.

Selected Bibliography: The Goalkeepers' History of Britain by Peter Chapman (Fourth Estate, 2008); Simple Goalkeeping Made Spectacular by Graham Joyce (Mainstream, 2009); In the Way! Goalkeepers – A Breed Apart? by Nick Hazlewood (Mainstream, 1998); The Outsider by Jonathan Wilson (Orion, 2013); The Guinness Book of Soccer Facts & Feats by Jack Rollin (Guinness, 1984); Only the Goalkeeper to Beat by Francis Hodgson (Picador, 1998).

Following the lead of author Rob Stokes, all the author royalties from Glove Story will be donated to Willow, the only UK charity supporting seriously ill 16 to 40 years old through Special Days. This donation represents the collective effort of the whole team of writers, photographers, illustrators, other individuals and businesses involved in the production of the book. You can find out more about Willow's work at willowfoundation.org.uk.

TEAMWORK

Grateful thanks to everyone who bought the *Glove Story* subscribers' package in advance. Your contribution has helped to launch Conker Editions, and hopefully we will now go on to publish many more books... ...

Paul Owens, East Yorkshire.

Jeff Sutherland, Islington.

Alan Thompsett, Redhill.

Matthew Lumb, Barnsley FC.

Dave Holmes, Caversham.

Lee Camp, Cardiff.

Stuart Hancocks, Wakefield.

Jamie Stephens, Totternhoe.

Jeff Maysh, Bromley.

Matthew Fox, Markyate.

Siôn Roberts, Anglesey.

Pete Weller, Molesey.

Vincenzo Portelli, Scicli.

Phil Williams, Bristol.

Duncan Burns, Cosham.

Martin Jarvis, Cambridge.

Viv O'Connor, Wicklow.

Rich Johnson, The Football Attic.

Eric Wu, Goalkeeper Sharing.

John Williams, Portsmouth.

Lee Roberts, PDMC.

Jim Stone, Waterlooville.

Ben Scott, Bournemouth.

Manfred Tschenett, Bolzano.

Stephen Taylor, Southsea.

Johan de Vicq, Maryland.

Danny Knight, Farlington.

Stephen Harley, Fife.

Sebastian Selke, Pimp My Gloves.

Ben Lewens, Wokingham.

Lee Renshaw, Corby.

Carl Alexander.

Nick Smith, Nottingham.

Andy Funnell, Happy 70th!

Mick and Rob Richards, Cosham.

Rod Brocksom, Portsmouth.

Gary Barnes, Bristol.

Frank Kerslake, Leicester.

Colin Murrant, Desborough.

Grant Comley, Cosham.

Lynne Harrison, Liverpool.

John Parker, Bristol.

Steve Patrick, Cosham.

Trevor Saunders, Great Yarmouth.

Tony Maddox, Stoke.

Jonathan Paardekooper, Waterlooville.

Ersin Akartuna, Croydon.

Dan Bean, London.

Tom Kristensen, Washington State.

Mark Allen, Bolton.

Gavin Haigh, Durham.

Chris Pinder.

Steve Stacy, Westgate on Sea.

Wayne Tomlinson, Doncaster.

Sam Yates, Lincolnshire.

Killian Kirrane, Dublin.

Mark Cannell, Portsmouth.

Pauline Atkinson, to Matthew.

Elaine Barton, Coventry.

Bill Batchelor, Waterlooville.

Stuart Ford, Stocksbridge.

Jamie O'Brien, Attenborough Colts.

Martin Keys, Twickenham.

Mark Chilab, London.

Matt Howarth, Portsmouth.

Neil Parkins, Portsmouth.

Paul Higgs, Havant.

David Battley, Chiswick.

Paul Thomas, Portsmouth.

James Culpin, Newcastle upon Tyne.

Ben Marlow, Mitcham.

Phil Ward, Emsworth.

Kevin Connolly, Glasgow.

Dennis McCafferty, East Lothian.

Stuart Page, Brough.

Olivia Paviour, Leigh-on-Sea.

Bradley Pike, Grassroots Goalies.

Eddie Silke, Leicester.

Alan Prigmore, Elstree.

Rich Molyneux, Havant.

Mark Buckingham, Leicester.

Sean Simpson, Portsmouth.

Team Trickett, Accrington.

Nathan Bennett, Dinas Powys.

Dominic Robbins, Misterton.

Karl Hanssens, Nieuwrode.